COMPASS GUIDE

A Strategic Plan For Goal Based Directional Living With A Godly Kingdom Purpose

By Dr. Daniel Daves

Paperback Workbook	ISBN #978-0-9763521-4-3
PDF Workbook	ISBN #978-0-9763521-5-0

© 2012 Mighty Eagle Publishing. All Rights Reserved under International Copyright Law. Printed in the United States of America. Contents and/or cover may not be reproduced in whole or in part in any form without the expressed written consent of the publisher. If you are interested in distribution rights for this book, contact info@mightyeagle.com or Mighty Eagle Publishing, P.O. Box 179, Mansfield, TX USA 76063. If a PDF or Kindle version is purchased, the purchaser may print one working copy for personal use and note taking. Not to be shared or re-printed without written consent from the publisher.

*Unless otherwise indicated, all scripture quotations are taken from the King James and New International Versions of the Bible.

Published By: Mighty Eagle Publishing

P.O. Box 179, Mansfield, TX 76063   Email: info@mightyeagle.com

Web Sites: www.mightyeagle.com   www.doctordanieldaves.com

Dr. Daniel Daves, PhD

Who Is Dr. Daniel Daves?

Dr. Daniel Daves is "The Giant Tracker™" and is involved in business development, education, and international philanthropic works. He speaks internationally as an author and professional, helping organizations and leaders to break the negative cycles of poverty, as well as, align correctly with God's miraculous rhythmic cycles of life, investment, and growth. He trains students how to successfully track the secret financial movements of markets, industries, businesses and governments. Dr. Daves has a Masters degree in Missiology, a D.Min and a PhD in Christian Administration from Logos Christian College & Graduate School, Jacksonville, FL. He has 32+ years of ministry and business experience in America and on the mission field. He is married to his wife Tracy and they have two wonderful children, Ariel & Danny.

You can find out more about Dr. Daniel Daves or contact him by checking out his website at www.doctordanieldaves.com. Dr. Daves is typically available for limited speaking engagements. This workbook can be used with a one/two day seminar which Dr. Daves presents online and internationally in person.

Table Of Contents

1. Are You Living An Accident Or On Purpose? — 7
2. Success Or Failure – Key Word "Obedience" To God Plan — 9
3. Three Dimensional Living That Most People Never Find — 13
4. Where Is Your Ship Headed? Short, Medium & Long Range Goals — 17
5. The Art Of Vision Casting (Excerpt From "The Business Of Ministry") — 21
6. Key: Commitment To Reading God's Word Daily — 25
7. Bringing Your Eight Life Provinces Under God's Kingdom Domain — 31
8. Journaling, Communicating, And Developing Your Life Goals — 35
9. Creating A Twenty Five Word "Core Life Purpose" Statement — 37
10. Final Instructions — 45
11. One Year Bible Reading Calendar — 47
12. Personal Territory Goals & Journaling Pages - Physical — 59
13. Personal Territory Goals & Journaling Pages - Mental — 87
14. Personal Territory Goals & Journaling Pages - Spiritual — 115
15. Personal Territory Goals & Journaling Pages – Social — 143
16. Personal Territory Goals & Journaling Pages - Educational — 171
17. Personal Territory Goals & Journaling Pages – Vocational — 199
18. Personal Territory Goals & Journaling Pages – Marital — 227
19. Personal Territory Goals & Journaling Pages - Financial — 255
20. Twenty Five Word "Focused Core Purpose Statement" — 283
21. Daily Goals & Notes Page To Copy — 284
22. Additional Notes — 291

In Honor & Memory Of Al Hopson

I would like to dedicate this workbook to the late Al Hopson who impacted my life as a young man. While I was youth pastoring a youth group in a small church in Kansas, Al accepted an invitation to come speak in our wheat field church. He was dynamic, filled with life and passion, and he delivered the message of God's kingdom in a new way that I could grasp.

Al spent multiple days laying the foundation for me so that I could bring my "whole man" under the kingdom of God. Twenty five years later, I have written this manual with updates, additions and modifications to filter and focus a person's future towards divine and eternal success. This plan has worked over the last 25 years in my own life, family, ministry, relationships and business ventures.

Al Hopson worked at Stanford University and he was known as a "Life Planner". His laughter was contagious. His message was riveting and purpose filled. His spirit projected Heaven's light and eternal life. He was filled with the love of Jesus. Thank you Al Hopson for laying the foundation for the next two generations in front of you! You have been greatly missed since passing to Heaven in 1990.

Sincerely,

Dr. Daniel Daves

Prov 13:22 (KJV) A good man leaveth an inheritance to his children's children: and the wealth of the sinner is laid up for the just.

What Can I Expect Through This Workbook?

Compass Guide is an ever expanding workbook study of your life, goals, visions, dreams, and talents. This workbook will teach you the biblical importance of goal setting. It will teach you how to dig deep and find God's intentional design for your life. You will learn how to unlock your vast, hidden potential. Then you will turn that potential into miraculous reality through the principles of "Filter & Focus", "Three Dimensional Living", "Constructive Journaling", and passing your life through the "Fires Of God".

Within one year of using this living workbook, you will have found your direction and focus for one, five, ten, twenty and even fifty years from now. Your compass direction will be charted and your focus will become clear.

With a solid commitment to God, reading His Holy Bible, and daily journaling/goal setting, you will enter a miraculous lifestyle of divine fulfillment, joy, and purpose. You will accomplish more than you could ever have imagined before. You will walk with God as friends and He will help you accomplish the impossible. You will join the ranks of noble kings who turn potential into manifest reality!

Welcome to "Compass Guide"!

Habakkuk 2:2 "Write the vision, and make it plain upon tables, that he may run that readeth it."

Chapter 1
Are You Living An Accident Or On Purpose?

God has created you in His own marvelous image by design and on purpose! What an awesome thought to know that God wants us to look, act, live and move just like He does. He is your Father in Heaven and He wants to help you to succeed in every area of life which He created you for. He is successful, creative, well informed, and He has a plan. He has principles and lives by rules and laws of success. He is perfect. He wants nothing less than the best for His children, who are royalty in His kingdom!

Unfortunately, many people are so disconnected from their Heavenly Father that they are living only in a shadow of God's reality that He has for them. They don't know His voice, His will or how He thinks. For this reason, many will perish and fall by the wayside of life never having known their true calling, purpose and identity. Graveyards around the world are filled with people who never planted their seed, who never pursued their dreams, and who wasted their life in purposeless, hopeless, cycles of futility and non productivity. You don't have to perish as they did.

Prov 29:18 (KJV) Where there is no vision, the people perish: but he that keepeth the law, happy is he.

Statistics say that a large percentage of the world's population has never made plans for their future. Very few have financial goals or any other goals for that matter. Some will set a short term goal to lose weight, or to get through college. But what about their five, ten, twenty or fifty year goals? For most, these goals are non-existent for a variety of reasons which you are going to overcome through this workbook. Most people don't understand the importance of connecting with almighty God to find their goals, purpose, and destiny on earth. Instead, they believe that luck, accidental success or hitting the lottery is the only way they can fall into prosperity. Therefore, they waste their lives and take God's ideas and plans into an early grave.

Jer 29:11-13 (NIV) For I know the plans I have for you," declares the LORD, "plans to prosper you and not to harm you, plans to give you hope and a future. Then you will call upon me and come and pray to me, and I will listen to you. You will seek me and find me when you seek me with all your heart.

God believes that goals are important. He has written history (His story) in the Holy Bible as a textbook for living. We can get to know Him, know His timeless ways and thoughts, and learn from the way He thinks, acts and plans. It's true that He is a goal setter, He makes plans, and He moves on His ideas. He knew you before He formed you, and He brought you to the earth for a very special purpose.

Jer 1:4-5 (NIV) The word of the LORD came to me, saying, "Before I formed you in the womb I knew you, before you were born I set you apart; I appointed you as a prophet to the nations."

God believes in counsel and planning. He believes in advisers and team members. God also believes in success, and He wants you to be successful in every area of life.

Prov 15:22 (NIV) Plans fail for lack of counsel, but with many advisers they succeed.

Many people have lots of ideas of how to prosper, how to build their lives, and how to do just about everything they want to do. However, God wants you to trust Him first of all, and to learn from Him in order to fulfill your life on earth. This is the best way to live with divine purpose and eternal value. This is the only way to please God and to succeed honestly and eternally.

Psalms 37:3-6 (NIV) Trust in the LORD and do good; dwell in the land and enjoy safe pasture. Delight yourself in the LORD and he will give you the desires of your heart. Commit your way to the LORD; trust in him and he will do this: He will make your righteousness shine like the dawn, the justice of your cause like the noonday sun.

God also believes that it's important to write down your vision, your plans, and your goals. There is something about writing it down and making it plain. A heavenly law is set into motion when a person correctly writes down God's vision for their lives. Heaven and earth come into agreement and Heaven's power, strength, and resources become available on the earth to the person who writes down their vision and goals in the proper manner. This workbook is going to help you to write your vision, goals, and priorities.

Hab 2:2-3 (KJV) And the LORD answered me, and said, Write the vision, and make it plain upon tables, that he may run that readeth it. For the vision is yet for an appointed time, but at the end it shall speak, and not lie: though it tarry, wait for it; because it will surely come, it will not tarry.

Psalms 119:105 (NIV) Your word is a lamp to my feet and a light for my path.

Seminar Notes For Chapter 1:

Chapter 2
Success Or Failure – Key Word "Obedience" To Gods Plan

God has a destiny for you which He purposed in His mind before you were born. He brought you to this earth at this time for this purpose. It's going to be up to you to find it, choose to follow it, submit to it, pursue it, and fulfill it. God will help you, but He will not do it for you while you watch on the sidelines. Why does He make you seek, find, and pursue His purpose and instructions? It's part of your training as a son, a king and a member of His royal family. This training will teach you to find all of God's secrets and hidden treasures in Heaven and on earth.

Many people are too hard headed and rebellious to choose God's plan for their lives, because they're filled with pride, arrogance, and false purpose and they're generally disconnected from a true relationship with God. These types of people will need to burn themselves out, fail miserably, hit the proverbial bottom of the barrel before they will look up, find God, and choose His plan for their lives. These people are all around us, and are in various stages of finding or denying their true identity and destiny. The good news for you is that you are seeking His plan and you have a workbook manual that will help you find that plan. I can assure you that you will find His plan inside of you. The code is inside your heart. This manual will help you to crack the code and reveal His plan for your life. You will not be disappointed! You will find joy, peace, excitement and true fulfillment when the plan miraculously unfolds in your life.

A Note From the author, Dr. Daniel Daves: "I was an arrogant, prideful fool who had my own plans and was hell bent on fulfilling my own desires as a teenager. It only took 18 years for me to totally wreck my life and come to utter destruction, drug and alcohol addiction, and jail time. I was finally at rock bottom with no relationship with God, a failure and a sinner. It was then that I called out to God who reached down with a hand of mercy and rescued me. I now live for Him and realize that His divine will is the one that I must always choose for the new life He gave me in Christ." – Dr. Daniel Daves

Psalms 40:1-3 (NIV) I waited patiently for the LORD; he turned to me and heard my cry. He lifted me out of the slimy pit, out of the mud and mire; he set my feet on a rock and gave me a firm place to stand. He put a new song in my mouth, a hymn of praise to our God.

Once a person submits to God and begins to seek Him with their whole heart, they will soon find that God's will is for the salvation of Jesus Christ to renew and restore mankind into God's true purpose. Without the salvation of Jesus Christ and the power of God's Holy Spirit moving in a person's life, there is no hope for honestly and eternally fulfilling God's will in a human being's life.

2 Peter 3:9 (NIV) The Lord is not slow in keeping his promise, as some understand slowness. He is patient with you, not wanting anyone to perish, but everyone to come to repentance.

Once the foundation of Christ's death, burial and resurrection life is correctly laid in a person's heart, then the house can be built correctly. But the new life that comes from receiving Jesus Christ as Lord and Savior is the absolute first step. Without this foundation, everything else will eventually fail. But if a person builds on this foundation correctly, it will result in a rock solid life that passes every test of life, and which becomes a blessing to God and man.

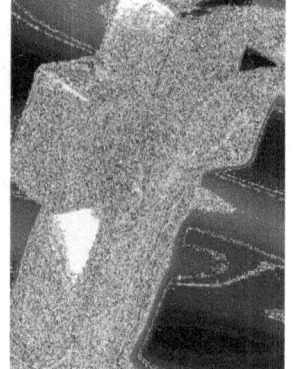

1 Cor 3:11 (NIV) For no one can lay any foundation other than the one already laid, which is Jesus Christ.

This workbook is assuming that you have laid the foundation of Christ in your life, and that your life and commitment is first and foremost to God and His way of building your life. With the foundation of Christ, let's start building.

There is an ancient saying which says, "When the student is ready, the teacher will appear." This profound statement can be used in any human scenario. A person must be hungry for God, thirsty for righteousness, humbled and poor in spirit, knowing that he or she is nothing without God's miraculous plan unfolding in their life. It's when the disciple is ready that our teacher, the powerful Holy Spirit, will appear. Are you ready?

God wants you to have vision, revelation, insight and special understanding, and He wants you to walk in a supernatural life that's different from others. You are going to receive timeless instruction from God's book of wisdom, the Holy Bible. You're going to hear His voice directing you. You're going to start activating your heart's desires and dreams in order to pursue and fulfill them. You will be different than others. While they waste away in aimlessness, false hopes, and useless dreams, you will be taking aim at your true destiny. While they waste their time and energy at the next party or the next social function, you will be living, moving and having your being "on purpose". You will set your sites, your goals, and your interests in a manner that your family, friends and co-workers may not understand or appreciate. But you will be leading the way into success and prosperity, and others will eventually follow and start asking questions as they see God's Kingdom working with you to perform the miraculous! This lifestyle will be nothing short of amazing. It will have bumps, setbacks and hurdles. But God will educate you and teach you through them all. You will overcome the world and learn to move mountains.

Psalms 34:19-20 (NIV) A righteous man may have many troubles, but the LORD delivers him from them all; he protects all his bones, not one of them will be broken.

God created Adam and then He gave him instructions for his life and the garden.

God gave Noah a multi-decade long, detailed set of instructions of how to move God's divine plan into the future, saving his own family members in the process.

God gave Moses detailed instructions on how to free Israel from their harsh slave masters and Pharaoh.

God showed Moses the details of His covenant with Israel and Moses carved the details of the Ten Commandments in stone.

God showed Moses in detail how to build the Ark of the Covenant and all of the pieces of the Tabernacle.

God gave Joshua insight and detailed daily instruction on how to rid the land of giants and establish Israel in the land of promise.

God gave King David specific instructions on how to defeat the enemy and build a successful kingdom.

God gave Solomon unfathomable wisdom to rule the people and become the wealthiest king in all of history.

God gave Jesus the detailed plans and wisdom to walk on earth as a man and fulfill His divine purpose of going to a horrible, harsh death on a cross, one time for all mankind.

God is the King of instruction and blessing. If He gave instruction to these people, He will do it for you as well. But there is a correct way to learn His instruction and an incorrect way. This workbook is positioned to help you be more successful than you could have ever imagined before. We will discuss the secrets to success in the next chapter.

Seminar Notes For Chapter 2

Habakkuk 2:2 "Write the vision, and make it plain upon tables, that he may run that readeth it."

Chapter 3
Three Dimensional Living That Most People Never Find

There are three dimensions in your life that God wants you to realize and benefit from. Yet most people never tap into any dimension past the first one. Therefore, they're unfulfilled and they never realize their hopes, desires, and dreams. They are held down to the first dimension and suffer from poverty and lack. Their hope is deferred and their hearts become sick. Their dreams eventually fade and their candle goes out. Many are held down in the first dimension and they die never having seen their land of promise!

Dimension #1: NEED

Dimension #2: DESIRE

Dimension #3: THE DREAM

Dimension One: NEED

*Phil 4:19 (NIV) And my God will meet **all your needs** according to his glorious riches in Christ Jesus.*

One of the powerful qualities of life with God is that He meets your needs. He is all powerful and meets needs that no human institution could ever meet. There is no structure on earth with the capacity to feed every animal on the planet for just one day. Yet, God feeds them every day. He also feeds and clothes you.

*Matt 6:25-33 (NIV) "Therefore I tell you, do not worry about your life, what you will eat or drink; or about your body, what you will wear. Is not life more important than food, and the body more important than clothes? Look at the birds of the air; they do not sow or reap or store away in barns, and yet your heavenly Father feeds them. Are you not much more valuable than they? Who of you by worrying can add a single hour to his life? "And why do you worry about clothes? See how the lilies of the field grow. They do not labor or spin. Yet I tell you that not even Solomon in all his splendor was dressed like one of these. If that is how God clothes the grass of the field, which is here today and tomorrow is thrown into the fire, will he not much more clothe you, O you of little faith? So do not worry, saying, 'What shall we eat?' or 'What shall we drink?' or 'What shall we wear?' For the pagans run after all these things, and your heavenly Father knows that you need them. **But seek first his kingdom and his righteousness, and all these things will be given to you as well.***

God is the master of meeting the needs of His creation. He even tells us to pray that He will meet those needs.

*Matt 6:9-11 (NIV) "'Our Father in heaven, hallowed be your name, your kingdom come, your will be done on earth as it is in heaven. **Give us today our daily bread.***

"Dimension One" is all about meeting needs. When you have a need for something, you can pray and ask God. He will help you get what you need. He will also use you to help meet others needs as you give to the poor, care for widows and orphans, and go on important missions trips to other far off lands where the people are calling out to God to meet their needs.

Once a person becomes born again, they will begin to see the love of God in action as He helps them in their infirmities, He meets their needs and heals their sicknesses through many different ways. It's a wonderful thing to have "Dimension One" in operation in your life. However, Dimension One can never bring you to your heart's desires, nor can it help you reach your dreams. These are two other dimensions that God wants you to pursue.

There is a difference between needs and desires. You can't use Dimension One to bring you into Dimension Two. You can't apply the promises of God for meeting your needs, and expect those promises to give you the desires of your heart. You're going to have to get into "Dimension Two" and find a new set of promises, principles, and laws to bring your heart's desires.

Later in this workbook, you will be writing down your life goals. Don't allow yourself to only write goals in "Dimension One". God will meet your needs. But He wants you to jump to Dimension Two and Dimension Three for the fulfillment of your goals and vision. While some goals you list may be Dimension One goals, plan to jump to Dimension Two and Three.

Dimension Two: DESIRE

*Psalms 37:4-6 (NIV) Delight yourself in the LORD and he will give you **the desires of your heart**. Commit your way to the LORD; trust in him and he will do this: He will make your righteousness shine like the dawn, the justice of your cause like the noonday sun.*

There's a huge difference between needs and desires. Just as a person needs vegetables to be healthy, he may DESIRE some ice cream or chocolate cake once in awhile. Many people need a car to get to work, but they really want a certain style, make and model of car. This is the difference between need and desire. The Holy Bible declares that God wants to give you the desires of your heart. There's a reason that you like certain things. God built those desires into you so that you will pursue them. While there are plenty of things that we need, we have certain desires that come alive when we see, taste, smell, touch and hear. We like certain music, certain foods and drinks, certain smells, certain sights and places to visit. This phenomenon is what makes each of us unique, just like a fingerprint.

God wants you to bring every desire of your life under self control. A rogue, out of control body, mind, emotion, or habit is very destructive to the purpose that God has for you. Therefore, Psalms 37 says to "Delight yourself in the Lord." Get into His life, His plan, and His kingdom. Drag any rogue, rebellious, out of control emotion or habit under the dominion of His Kingdom. When you do this and develop a lifestyle of keeping yourself pure, you will see God as He gives you the desires of your heart. Self control is the key to Dimension Two. A lifestyle of restraint and self control is the secret key to Dimension Two being unlocked in your life.

Imagine having God GIVE YOU the desires of your heart. Now we're talking FUN! This is the place that most people never get to because they're lazy, unrestrained, undisciplined and unholy. They never experience Dimension Two and they are never fulfilled in their lives. They never set goals, and they have no target to shoot for. They never "plan" to find Dimension Two, and they are surely not going to find it. While many people are just one lifestyle change away from a miraculous new dimension, most will never take the step forward to become a disciple, a disciplined one, and they will not delight themselves in the Lord as Psalms 37 commands.

As part of your goals and vision, plan to overcome any bad habits, to discipline yourself, and stop living lazily off of Dimension One. Ask God to help you overcome and put your old fleshly habits to death. Ask Him to show you how to delight yourself IN HIM, so that you can live in Dimension Two.

While this is an awesome dimension that few ever find, this isn't the last dimension for you to enjoy. There is one more dimension. Even fewer people will find this dimension, as it requires a total make over. This total make over is what you're headed for in this workbook! Dimension Three is your target!

Dimension Three: THE DREAM

*Eph 3:20-21 (KJV) Now unto him that is able to do **exceeding abundantly above all that we ask or think**, according to the power that worketh in us, Unto him be glory in the church by Christ Jesus throughout all ages, world without end. Amen.*

"Dimension Three" is dream land. This is the place where only a few find during their lives. This is the final culmination and target. Paul said, *"I have fought a good fight, I have finished my course, I have kept the faith." (2 Tim. 4:7).* Finishing your course in faith will bring you to THE DREAM, or dream land.

Have you ever heard someone who says about their job, "I can't believe that they pay me to do this job. I love doing this so much that I would do it for free if they refused to pay me!". These people have excitement and zeal in them, and they're projecting joy, power and fulfillment everywhere they go. These people have found their dream, or at least a portion of it. God wants you to experience this in your life as well.

There are many obstacles to living THE DREAM. Some are put up intentionally by God to educate you and build strength into your life. Those who live in dream land will need to fight to stay there. Israel's dream land was the land of promise (Canaan) which was filled with giants. Not only would Israel have to kill them all and take their territory, they would have to learn to live successfully in this new dimension of giants. Training would be needed, as well as extreme adherence to God's plan and His voice. They would have to leave their life and understanding as slaves, and start to walk and live as kings and conquerors. It would require a total make over. Unfortunately, the first Israelite generation could not grasp Dimension Three. They stumbled in Dimension One for forty years until they died in the wilderness unfulfilled. But their offspring would raise up in the wilderness to seize Dimension Three. This generation actually believed that God's long awaited promise was for them. They believed that their God was big enough to give them the land that He promised for centuries to their people. They activated their faith, started thinking like kings instead of slaves, and they seized the land with God's guidance, instruction, leadership, and help.

Remember when Israel crossed over to the land of promise as they prepared to seize their dream? They were circumcised, went through intense pain, and were commanded to listen to every word that Joshua spoke. They would do seemingly pointless activities like march around the city for seven days. They would blow trumpets. They would shut their mouths until it was time to talk. They learned obedience, and whenever disobedience appeared, the entire nation lost their ability to live in dream land. Achan disobeyed God and it affected the entire nation. Many of the Israelites died in battle at Ai because of Achan's disobedience.

You are going to learn through this workbook to bring every area of your life under God's Kingdom domain. More on this later. If you are successful at the end of this workbook training, you will begin to see and live in Dimension Three. It won't be easy to cross over into it, but it will be worth it! Just to see this dimension is a powerful thing. But to enter it is literally a "Dream Come True"! God will give you a dream. He will then help you to pursue it. With faith and perseverance, you will step into it and inherit that dream!

Dimension Three is dream land. Everyone has a dream at some point in their lives, but conflict, laziness or lack of training can extinguish the dream and lock a person back into Dimension One only. But dream land is the land of inheritance. Here you can inherit ripened fields that you didn't plant and live in houses that you didn't have to build. You become an heir of lands, businesses, properties, ministries, and you begin to inherit God's Kingdom, learning to rule it as a king. You will love your life, family, career and surroundings so much that people around you will realize that you are living in Dimension Three, your dream land.

This workbook will help you to distinguish and identify "Dream Thieves" which are all around you. From well meaning family members to friends and business partners, dream thieves can be all around you. Identifying your core purpose in life and setting your goals will help you filter out the dream thieves and keep them far away from you. Dream thieves come to pull you off course, to try to intimidate you, and to reduce your faith in your vision and dream. Most of the time, they don't realize that they're working against you. They're just operating under the wrong spirit of poverty and lack.

Paul identifies dream thieves as he points out those inside and outside the church who live as enemies of the cross. They may even be born again, but in their actions, cravings, and desires, they are enemies of dream land.

Phil 3:18-19 (NIV) For, as I have often told you before and now say again even with tears, many live as enemies of the cross of Christ. Their destiny is destruction, their god is their stomach, and their glory is in their shame. Their mind is on earthly things.

You will identify these dream thieves quickly as you progress forward with this workbook. God wants you to pursue the dream, and to identify the dream thieves quickly. Can you think of any dream thieves that stand opposed to you at this time? Write down the obvious dream thieves that you currently recognize.

Seminar Notes For Chapter 3

_____

_____

_____

_____

_____

_____

Habakkuk 2:2 "Write the vision, and make it plain upon tables, that he may run that readeth it."

Chapter 4

Where Is Your Ship Headed? Short, Medium, And Long Range Goals

Just imagine that your family is on their way to a one week cruise to the Caribbean. When you arrive at the port, you sit in a meeting with your ship's captain. He seems like a captain because he's wearing the uniform. However, when he begins to speak, he reveals some startling information of great concern to you and your family.

"Hello ladies and gentlemen and welcome aboard. I am your captain, Jonathon Risktaker. I will be your leader on this seven to nine day journey. Once we get you all aboard, we will be taking off from the port. We hope to get out to sea by sunset but there are no guarantees. I know the brochure said that you would see the sun set from the ocean, but the crew had a few things they forgot for the trip and they might be late getting them loaded this afternoon. We'll see what we can do. Now the Caribbean is full of wonderful islands, and we are going to try to cruise to at least three of them this week. If we have time, we will go to four islands. I'm not sure which one we will get to first, as I don't have a map on this trip. We're going to trust the stars for our direction at night, and we will use the sun by day. Please pray that there are no clouds this week for our night travel. By the way, has anyone heard the weather report for the week in the Caribbean? Please enjoy yourselves and have a great cruise with us this week. We will do our best to be back at this port in seven to nine days. If we run too late, we will find another dock to end the cruise somewhere along this coast. Thank you for sailing with us!"

Now if you have any wisdom at all, you are not going to get on this cruise ship. This captain is not prepared, he has not planned, and he doesn't have a map or directions. This cruise is headed for disaster, and you don't want to be anywhere near this failed voyage, or its captain.

The captain who sets no goal for his ship will surely not hit it! No one hits a goal that they fail to set!

Most of us would never get on a cruise ship with a captain like this. However, most of us work at jobs around people who are sailing their ships just like this captain. We go to school with them, we work with them, we live among them and we go to church with them. Many of us serve under church leaders who have no vision or purpose. Remember, if you are serving in their church, or giving your time, talent, skill, and future into their programs, businesses or ministries, you are a traveler on their ship. They are the captain and you are going where they're going. Are you sure that you want to go where they are going? If they have no real plans, vision, goals, or agenda, they are absolutely dead in the water. You will be dead in the water with them. You may want to reconsider who you are following, working for, or giving your life to. A person can never go farther than their captain. Maybe you need to get another captain and find another ship. When you're on another man's bus, you are going where he is taking you. Make sure he is going where you are going.

It's vitally important that you submit to the command of God to have goals, vision, and written plans. Don't waste another fruitless day without pursuing this kind of life. And don't waste your time serving under people who will lead you nowhere.

Everyone needs short, medium, and long term goals. We need daily goals in order to measure our daily creativity. We need weekly, monthly, and yearly goals. We need a five year, ten year, twenty year, and fifty year plan. Building this plan will force you to dig deep into your life, heart, desires, and dreams. You will be driven to talk with God about the future and to press into His wisdom and direction for your life. It's not easy, but it's worth it. Success is not easy, and nothing eternal is easy. Nothing eternal will happen without planning. This workbook will teach you how to develop short, medium, and long term plans for your life.

FILTER & FOCUS

A detailed set of goals and plans will help you to FILTER and FOCUS. These are two of the most important words you will ever know and use in planning and developing.

1. Filter out all of the non profitable things from your life which steal your attention, your strength, and your capacity to accomplish your goals. Harness yourself and restrict yourself away from fruitless deeds, sinful activities, pointless relationships, and anything that detracts from your life with God and your divine purpose on earth.

2. Focus on what is important, not on what's urgent. Urgencies will always come. But your focus needs to be sharp and serious, like the stare of an eagle. Set your eyes on your short, medium, and long range goals and don't get distracted. Remain single minded, with your eyes set and focused on the short, medium, and long term goals that God will help you build for your life. With focus, you will succeed and find a way. With focus you will overcome any mountain and will walk in the miraculous.

FILTER and FOCUS will only work if you build correctly through goal setting and vision casting.

A purpose filled life doesn't happen by chance or accident. And a person doesn't get lucky on purpose. However, bad luck, poverty, trouble and a curse comes on people who don't discipline themselves to filter, focus, vision cast, and set divinely inspired goals. Today, you will begin a journey of FILTER and FOCUS.

There's a saying that "It's the foxes that spoil the vine." This is so true as we all have non profitable things in our lives which distract us from reality, from what's important, and from our true goals and purpose. Some people are so hopelessly diffused from reality that they spend 90%

of their lives doing things that will amount to nothing. They spend less than 10% of their lives doing what is important, eternal, and directed towards their goals. Many people respond to urgencies rather than what's important. But a person who is disciplined knows that he or she must do what's important, not what's urgent. It's the urgencies of the day that will steal your vision, your accomplishments, and your purpose in life. Do what's important. Filter out all of the non profitable things from your life that are holding you back, stealing your time, and stealing your purpose. Filter, filter, filter!

Focus is important. Not only must we focus on what's important, but we must focus on the right things. Here's a brief story from www.goal-setting-for-success.com :

THE POWER OF FOCUS: Most of us never really focus because we don't know the power of focus. We constantly feel a kind of irritating psychic chaos because we keep trying to think of too many things at once. There's always too much up there on the screen.

There was an interesting motivational talk on this subject given by former Dallas Cowboys coach Jimmy Johnson to his football players:

" I told them that if I laid a two-by four plank across the room, everybody there would walk across it and not fall, because our focus would be that we were going to walk that two-by-four. But if I put that same two-by-four plank 10 stories high between two buildings only a few would make it, because the focus would be on failing. Focus is everything. The team that is more focused today is the team that will win this game."

Johnson told his team not to be distracted by the crowd, the media, or the possibility of losing, but to focus on each play of the game itself just as if it were a good practice session.

The Cowboys won the game by 52-17.

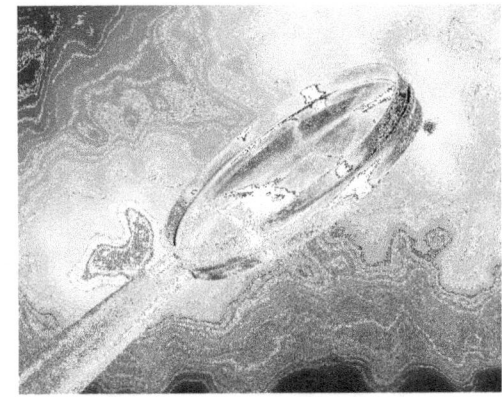

Focus takes discipline. If you can bring your thoughts, your time, and your attention into a focused, directional plan, you will cut through opposition like a laser beam! A magnifying glass can focus the sun's energy to a point to where normal sunlight can burn wood, melt glass and even melt rock when focused correctly. Your focus on your goals and direction will create the same intensity, passion and capacity to burn through any opposition that stands in your way.

If you focus on problems, the mountain in front of you, or your opposition, you will empower that area that is receiving your attention. But if you focus on your goals, you will empower those goals and bring great energy and strength to those goals. It's simply amazing, and it's true.

FILTER & FOCUS!

Seminar Notes For Chapter 4

Habakkuk 2:2 "*Write the vision, and make it plain upon tables, that he may run that readeth it.*"

Chapter 5
The Art Of Vision Casting

Here is an excerpt from one chapter in my book, "The Business Of Ministry" concerning vision casting and developing a long term plan, modified for this workbook.

VISION CASTING

DEVELOPING AND WORKING THE LONG TERM PLAN

It is so vitally important to have personal long term goals as well as church/ministry/business/professional long term goals. We must work our vision and purpose every day. Repetition and focus are the keys to success in God's ministry, business, and any endeavor you put your hands and time to. However, if we don't VISION CAST or keep our eye on the horizon with long term goals in mind, we can lose track of the true purpose of our ministry, business, job, family, etc. I know many people who have lost 5 – 10 years of their lives (or longer) because they failed to look forward into their future. They were so busy building the daily road and they never looked up to see if they were building it straight. They built themselves right into a dead end ally with no place to go.

You might be performing daily business or ministry assignments, and your schedule might be set for the next year with your computer ringing bells and whistles every day. You might have your routine set each day for the rest of your life, and that's important. However, if you don't have the larger picture in mind while you do these things, you will most certainly build off course and off of your true destiny.

Vision casting is vitally important to hitting your target goal. Where do you plan to be in 20 years? What goals, desires and dreams do you plan to have accomplished by then? What are some of the amazing things that you want to accomplish which will take the next 20 years of planning? Keep these things in front of you and remind yourself of them at least weekly.

Your daily and weekly grind of work, business, or ministry MUST be building towards your 20 and 50 year personal, family and business goals. If not, then you are building yourself into a dead end alley. There will be a day that you wake up and realize that your life is coming to an end and you are nowhere near your final purpose in life and ministry. Vision Casting will help you to keep the dream before your weekly, monthly and yearly view. You don't know what your

20 year plans, desires and dreams are? It's time to fast and pray, write down your goals and dreams and get the plan from God who gives freely to all who ask.

GOAL SETTING: PERSONAL, JOB, FAMILY, BUSINESS & MINISTRY EVALUATION

It's very important as a leader that you learn to set and define goals for your personal life, professional life, and ministry. I've heard that 90% of the world doesn't set goals while 10% of the world does set goals. The result is that 10% of the world owns 90% of the world's wealth and riches. Don't be another failed person in this world who fits into the 90% category. Your church people, business partners, co-workers and family need a leader who can teach and disciple them to become goal setters. No one deserves to be led down the road of poverty and lack. You're the one who must rise to the occasion, set and maintain your goals, and teach your staff and people to also set and maintain goals for their lives.

Psa 37:4-5 Delight thyself also in the LORD; and he shall give thee the desires of thine heart. Commit thy way unto the LORD; trust also in him; and he shall bring it to pass.

Goals are closely related to vision. They're a future vision cast of what is to come. None of us know exactly what is coming in the future, but we do know that God puts desires in our hearts so that we will chase after them. Therefore, your desires and dreams are closely related to God's divine will in your life. You must learn to focus, discipline, and restrain them under His direction and leading.

Take time and begin to dream. Write down your goals, desires, and dreams for the next one, five, ten, twenty, and fifty years. Remember that many Japanese business people plan for 150 years from now. Many of them are working their great grandfather's vision right now. You're only starting with a fifty year plan that's still within your own generation. We have a long way to go, so lets get started.

Don't be afraid to dream and vision cast. Your fulfillment in life will include reaching your goals and dreams. If you don't have any active goals set, you're surely not going to hit them. I can guarantee that the captain of a large ship will never hit the port of his dreams if he doesn't make some plans to sail that way. You're sure to never hit the goals that you never set.

You are going to have an opportunity in the back of this workbook to list multiple short, medium and long term goals for different areas of your life. As an exercise in future vision casting, start today by listing ten personal goals for your life which are important to you. If you are under 18 years old, write down five top personal goals. These goals need to be accomplished within the next 5 years. Try to list them in order of importance. Take some quality time with this. Pray and ask God to stir up your desires and dreams. Write these goals down with as much clarity and detail as possible. Choose your words carefully. You will have an opportunity to list goals for your family, work or ministry later in this workbook. Focus on personal goals in this section.

My top ten personal goals for the next five years:

1._____

2._____

3._____

4._____

5._____

6._____

7._____

8._____

9._____

10._____

This is only an exercise, but you will be able to use these goals later on in the workbook.

Once you pray over your goals and set them into place, you now have something to shoot for as an individual, a business leader, or a ministry leader. Meet frequently with your family, co-workers, business partners or staff to see what needs to be done next to reach these goals. Take pro-active steps to accomplish these goals. Ask God to open doors for you. Make decisions in light of your goals. Don't get side tracked and off course. You will look at your one and five year goals daily. Look at your ten year goals weekly, and your 20 and 50 year goals monthly. Always set each day to do something towards your goals. Build with consistency, discipline, and fervency.

As you get further revelation from God you might need to modify a goal. Go ahead and do it. However, keep the goals in front of you and get your entire family, co-workers, staff and team working daily to fulfill these goals. Imagine the multiplication of having your entire focus group working daily to accomplish your vision and goals. You'll be amazed at the corporate power of one! If one hundred can put ten thousand to flight, then imagine what you all can do together!!!

Lev 26:8 And five of you shall chase an hundred, and an hundred of you shall put ten thousand to flight: and your enemies shall fall before you by the sword.

I believe that goal setting is a very important part of character building, discipline and leadership. None of your family members, church people or staff (including yourself) deserve to be in the 90% category of people who don't set goals and who end up with minimal fulfilled destiny. You must get your team into the top 10% category. Start today and never stop!

Once you get used to working a 20 and 50 year plan, you need to consider a realistic 150 year plan which will span the lives of your children, grandchildren and great grandchildren. This will give you true multi-generational purpose and will absolutely change the way you make decisions, spend your time and focus your energies on earth.

Prov 13:22 (KJV) A good man leaveth an inheritance to his children's children: and the wealth of the sinner is laid up for the just.

If it's true that a good man leaves an inheritance for two generations ahead of him, then you need to hit God's target of being a good man. Take a moment right now and write a paragraph that states your dream for your next two future generations and what you want to see them doing with the anointing, wisdom, vision and knowledge that you've imparted into them.

Seminar Notes For Chapter 5

Chapter 6
Key: Commitment To Reading God's Word Daily

As we begin the journey of filtering and focusing, goal setting and vision casting, you must establish your life and build it correctly. The only sure way to learn from God and His divine thinking means that you must read and study the Holy Bible each and every day. This is the instruction book of wisdom, history and the way that God rules, judges and builds things. This book will teach you how He thinks, acts, speaks, and moves. It's the most important book in the world. It's literally alive, the words are living, and they will change you when you read them!

Heb 4:12 (NIV) For the word of God is living and active. Sharper than any double-edged sword, it penetrates even to dividing soul and spirit, joints and marrow; it judges the thoughts and attitudes of the heart.

The Holy Bible is the only book in the world that's alive. This is why the devil and his minions are always trying to keep the Bible away from people. It's illegal to hold a Holy Bible in many parts of the world, and owning one could get you killed if you fall into the hands of evil men. Satan knows that the Holy Bible brings light, life, and God's will on the earth. The Holy Bible brings liberty and freedom, and people who read the Holy Bible are hard to control, and not easily enslaved. Once the Holy Bible gets inside of a person, it changes them, awakens them, and raises them up to an understanding of who they are. Their identity crisis ends and their kingly personhood begins to emerge. This is why the Holy Bible, God's living and breathing word, is so dangerous and powerful against the powers of darkness and the plans of evil.

Since this is the most powerful book in the world, don't you think it's time to make a commitment to yourself and to God to read the Holy Bible each and every day of your life?

When a person has a transforming occurrence in his life called the "Born Again" experience, that person becomes a brand new person and the old person that they used to be dies, passes away, and perishes.

*2 Cor 5:17 (KJV) **17** Therefore if any man be in Christ, he is a new creature: old things are passed away; behold, all things are become new.*

A "Born Again" experience will dramatically affect your life, future, and goals because you have become translated out of the world of darkness and into His everlasting Kingdom of light. The difference of the two worlds is literally as night and day or darkness to light. Therefore, as you begin to live in this brand new

"Kingdom of light" experience, the old life will show dramatic signs of perishing, and the new life in Christ will show signs of life. You have entered a process that will require time, and which can be accelerated by thrusting yourself into the daily reading of God's living Word.

1 Peter 1:23 (NIV) For you have been born again, not of perishable seed, but of imperishable, through the living and enduring word of God.

Your goals, views, ideas and thinking will begin to change once you have had a true "Born Again" experience into the Kingdom of God and you begin to read His living Word.

Romans 12:2 (NIV) Do not conform any longer to the pattern of this world, but be transformed by the renewing of your mind. Then you will be able to test and approve what God's will is--his good, pleasing and perfect will.

The old patterns of this world will begin to fade, fail and no longer function for you once you have had a "Born Again" experience into the Kingdom of God. This is a very powerful process, yet it can be frustrating during times of change.

Personal Story From Author Dr. Daniel Daves: "When I became "Born Again" with a radical, life changing experience at age 18, everything changed. My surroundings changed, my friends changed, my habits and lifestyle changed, and more. God literally cleansed me from an old life, filled with old addictions and desires. I took on a new craving for the Holy Spirit, a desire to draw near to Jesus, and to learn anything I could about God's Kingdom and this new life I was immersed in.

During the next seven years of my life, I would be reading the Holy Bible almost every day. I asked questions, wore out three bibles in seven years, highlighted anything that moved in those pages, and I had a hunger and thirst for knowledge. But I was also somewhat of a goal setter.

I remember clearly back in those days of 1980 – 1986, as I would write down my annual goals at the beginning of January. Each year I would write down a list of things that I really wanted to get done. But with the new "Born Again" experience, I started noticing something terribly wrong. I found it increasingly difficult to reach my goals each year. I remember towards year five, six and seven that I would laugh and say to myself, "Why are you even writing these goals down, Daniel? God is not going to allow you to reach them!" It was a point of real frustration at times because I heard successful people commanding me to write down my goals for success. I had always tried to have goals in front of me. But suddenly it wasn't working out so well, and the only thing I could figure out was that I was now "Born Again" and something in this new kingdom of light was stopping me from reaching my old goals. But I started noticing that the new goals that were being birthed and created in me as I prayed and read the Bible were starting to be reached. I was crossing over into a new kingdom and I was being renewed by God's Holy Spirit day by day. I was starting to take on a new set of goals and direction for my life. The old life was passing away along with its goals. My old purpose was dead, and a new purpose in Christ was arising within me."

Jesus told Peter about the same issue in his own life.

John 21:18-19 (NIV) I tell you the truth, when you were younger you dressed yourself and went where you wanted; but when you are old you will stretch out your hands, and someone else will dress you and lead you where you do not want to go." Jesus said this to indicate the kind of death by which Peter would glorify God. Then he said to him, "Follow me!"

Peter learned that when he was young, he did what he wanted. However, as he began to mature in the faith and in the Kingdom of God, he would be led by another into places that he wouldn't necessarily go on his own. He would begin to fulfill goals and a vision that didn't come from him, but from God. He would take on another life and another set of directives for his life. Jesus told him how to accomplish these new goals through two simple words, "FOLLOW ME".

A "Born Again" experience will bring the same change to your life. As the Kingdom of God invades your life, and as the Word of God begins to breathe life into you, your mind will change. Your goals will begin to change. Your outlook and directives in life will re-focus. You will begin to see things the way Jesus sees them. You will have an increased capacity to "Follow Him" and know why you are following Him. This monumental life shift will dramatically impact your life, outlook, and goals. Frustrations can develop when you see the old goals, dreams, passions and desires passing away and remaining unfulfilled. But be encouraged, because the Kingdom of God is working in you, and a new blueprint of goals, priorities, and His vision is being worked into your core being. These core beliefs and goals will end up focusing you on God's divine and eternal plan for your life. They will change you from a darkened worldling to a light filled son of God.

Romans 8:14 (NIV) because those who are led by the Spirit of God are sons of God.

Romans 8:19 (NIV) The creation waits in eager expectation for the sons of God to be revealed.

Now that you know there is a process of transformation and a rebooting of your core beliefs, it's easy to see why we must immerse ourselves into the Word of God daily. God's word is like strong medicine which will permeate our being and restore us to health. It's like water which hydrates every cell in your body so it can function properly. It's like vinegar which will turn your cucumber into a delicious pickle. It's like a powerful nutritional supplement which will feed you what is needed to give you optimum strength. You will absolutely see the difference once you develop a desire, a taste, and a habit of devouring God's holy, living, eternal Word.

From Author, Dr. Daniel Daves: "A man who has brought tremendous hope, help, and change to believers through decades of teaching is Tom Leding. This man changed my life, ministry, and everything about my present and future once I met him and received from his ministry. I had spent years reading God's Word, going to bible college, pastoring, preaching messages, and being a student of the Word. However, I had never developed a rock solid plan of "how to" commit myself and the first part of my day to the Word of God. I never had a solid structure that would help me, my family, and my church to stay focused on daily reading of the Holy Bible.

One day I met Dr. Tom Leding who came to our church by divine appointment, to bring us into order and set us on a new course and path for our lives. Tom is the former chief accountant for American Airlines and a top salesman for Farmer's Insurance Company among 14,000 agents. He has an impeccable ministry and message, and we were so amazingly blessed that he would be willing to come to our little church in St. Louis and speak to us. We hung on to every word. By the end of his seminar and services, he had shown us a very simple, yet explosively powerful way to accelerate our lives in Christ. It was called, "The Five O'clock Club"

The Five O'clock Club is a simple way to say, "The First Part Of Your Day". He showed us a simple strategy to read the entire Bible in one year, and to read Psalms and Proverbs 12 times per year. The plan is simple: Two Old Testament chapters, two New Testament chapters, five Psalms and five Proverbs per day. A daily commitment to read the Bible through in one year using this model would dramatically change your life, bring newly opened doors, open a window of divine prosperity over your life, and change everything around you as the living Word of God invades your life.

Our church took his 30 day challenge and began a daily reading of the Word of God, putting that reading first in our day. If a person woke up at five o'clock, that's when the reading began. If a person worked a second evening shift and gets up at 11 a.m., that's when the reading began. Within 30 days, the individuals, families and our local church all received miraculous blessings from God, received divinely inspired ideas, and had family members come to Christ who had never known Him before. It was miraculous!

I recommend that you join Dr. Leding's Five O'clock Club, listen to his videos and read his books. His first 'must read" book is "From Rags To Riches". Find him at www.tomleding.com .

Dr. Leding has authorized us to put his daily bible reading calendar in chapter eleven of this manual. This twelve month calendar will help keep you on track to read the Bible all the way through in one year, and you will read Psalms and Proverbs twelve times per year. I believe that this is important because Psalms and Proverbs were written by kings. King David and King Solomon, the wisest king in the history of the world, have offered their input into your life. Read their books twelve times per year and you will begin to think like a king! This is God's desire."

Rev 5:10 (KJV) And hast made us unto our God kings and priests: and we shall reign on the earth.

If you are going to reach your God given, divine destiny, target and mark, don't you think it's imperative that you accelerate the core change inside of you? Apply the living, sharp, active, two edged sword, Word of God to your life every day. I can personally guarantee that applying the Holy Bible to the first part of your daily walk will change you dramatically, quickly, and powerfully. You will begin to have Heaven's vision and goals for your life in a way that you've never thought, dreamed or imagined before!

Eph 3:20-21 (NIV) Now to him who is able to do immeasurably more than all we ask or imagine, according to his power that is at work within us, to him be glory in the church and in Christ Jesus throughout all generations, for ever and ever! Amen.

Consider signing this agreement before God in the presence of Heaven and the Holy Angels.

Official Agreement Of Commitment

My Heavenly Father, I come to you in the name of Jesus my savior. I believe that your Holy Bible is a gift into my life. I believe that it is an important part of my life, and that it will help me to grow, to change, and to understand your love, your kingdom, your thoughts, and ways. I am making a commitment directly to you to take the next 12 months and read the Holy Bible at the beginning of each day. I ask you for help, guidance and continual reminder of my commitment to you as I fulfill my duty to your Word. I ask for Heaven's help to develop a positive habit in reading your Word at the beginning of each day. If for any reason I miss a day of reading, I will make that day up the very next day by doubling my reading for that day. I will fulfill my commitment to you, and I fully expect that your Holy Bible will change me from the inside, outward. I thank you for your help, your grace, and your empowerment to consume the entire Bible in one year, and to learn from Psalms and Proverbs twelve times per year. I am making this commitment for your glory and for your Kingdom, in Jesus' name, Amen.

Signed this _____ (day) day of _____(month and year).

_____   _____

Signature   Printed Name

If you have made the supreme commitment to read the Holy Bible every day for the next year, you are to be commended and congratulated. You are joining many others who have this same manual around the world, and who are reading the exact same scripture verses along with you each day. You have committed to take your life, goals, vision, and future through the fire of Heaven so that you can be purified, cleansed, purged, and made valuable. Just as gold or silver is refined and made valuable in the fire, you are now going to refine your life, goals, and future.

Mal 3:3-4 (NIV) He will sit as a refiner and purifier of silver; he will purify the Levites and refine them like gold and silver. Then the LORD will have men who will bring offerings in righteousness, and the offerings of Judah and Jerusalem will be acceptable to the LORD, as in days gone by, as in former years.

Heaven's fire is a purging and cleansing fire. It will perfect and refine you. When you submit your plans to the Holy Bible and God's eternal will, you will see amazing things happen as God refines you. Without a doubt, your plans will modify, change, and expand when you submit yourself to God's Word and the cleansing fire from Heaven.

The Hebrews Shadrach, Meshach, and Abednego were thrown into a fiery furnace which had been heated seven times hotter than normal. They were tied, bound and thrown in the furnace because they refused to worship Nebuchadnezzar's god. The soldiers who threw them in were killed by the blast of the flames at the opening of the furnace. But when these three men landed in the furnace, a fourth man appeared with them in the flames. No doubt, this man was Jesus. Even the king's advisers said that this fourth man looked like the son of God. The only thing that burned inside that furnace were the ropes that had these men bound. They were all walking around inside the fire freely! No doubt, when they were called out of the fire by the king, he had a different attitude about them. Not a hair on their heads was singed. Their robes were not scorched, and there was no smell of fire on them. They came out with power, with a message, and with the full attention of the king who worshipped their God on this day. Notice also that the fourth man in the fire never came out. He's still in the fire, waiting for us.

Heb 12:28-29 (NIV) Therefore, since we are receiving a kingdom that cannot be shaken, let us be thankful, and so worship God acceptably with reverence and awe, for our "God is a consuming fire."

When you submit yourself to a daily dose of the purifying, cleansing Word of God, you are getting in the fire with Jesus. You will only have your bonds and ropes burned off. You will not be hurt by the fire. Your vision and goals will be expanded. God will take you from small thinking to large thinking. He will show you the truth like you've never known before. Your old walls, barriers, hindrances, weaknesses, sins, and shortcomings will be burned away. This will make you much more valuable in the Kingdom of God, and your golden goals and vision will become 99.9% pure or higher!

Run to God. Run into the holy fire of God's Word. Let His fire cleanse and purify you for the next year on a daily basis. You will not be ashamed or disappointed!

Note: See the forum at www.doctordanieldaves.com to join daily bible devotions & comments.

Chapter 7
Bring Your Whole Man *"Eight Life Territories"* Under Gods Kingdom Domain

You spent some time practicing to write out your personal life goals in Chapter Five. But now you are going to learn to drill down where life really counts. This is the section that most people will never unfold in their lives. However, when you understand the facts behind this chapter, you will begin to see the powerful unfolding of God's miraculous plan in your whole person.

When God created Adam in the garden, He gave him a dominion mandate.

Gen 1:28 (KJV) And God blessed them, and God said unto them, Be fruitful, and multiply, and replenish the earth, and subdue it: and have dominion over the fish of the sea, and over the fowl of the air, and over every living thing that moveth upon the earth.

God has commanded man to **be faithful, multiply, replenish the earth, subdue it and have dominion**.

This manual is going to help you to develop these five priorities in your life. Having dominion will be a major part of developing a successful Christian life. This means that you will act like a king, and that you will be faithful over the domain which has been given to you. Every king has a domain. You have a domain with territories that you must have dominion over. This is part of your training to become a king in God's Kingdom.

We know that God has given a life garden to you, which can be divided into some key territories for understanding. Your life is an amazing kingdom domain. God wants you to rule this kingdom well, to make it multiply, and keep it safe. You will need to bring all of your kingdom territories under your care, to educate them, make them fruitful, make them multiply, and have dominion over them. We have verified at least eight territories in your life that you will need to subdue, bring under your care, protect, and multiply.

1. Physical
2. Mental
3. Spiritual
4. Social
5. Educational
6. Vocational
7. Marital
8. Financial

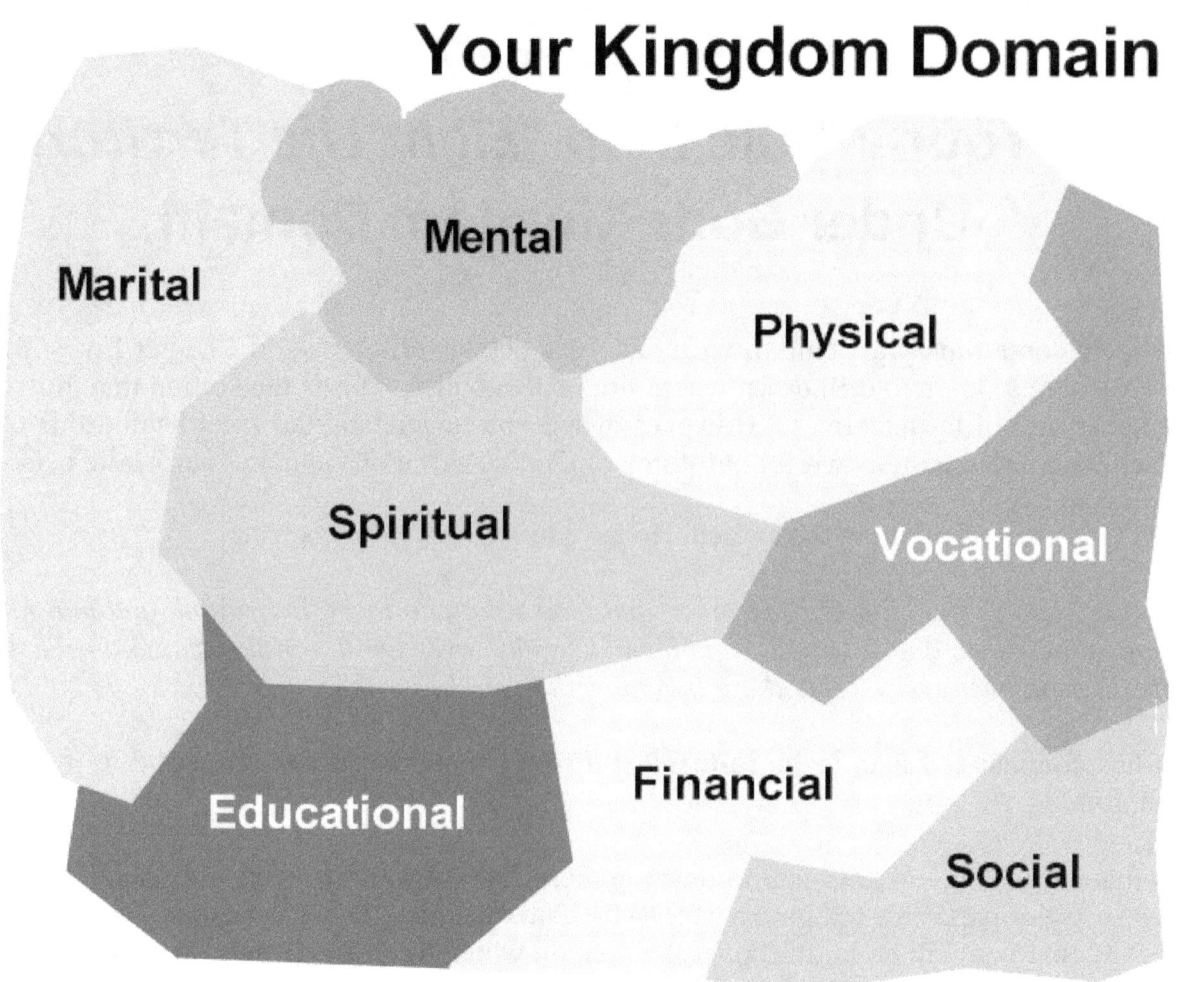

Your Kingdom Domain

Let's imagine for a moment that God has given you a kingdom to rule as part of your training. This kingdom has eight different territories, each with different strengths and weaknesses. Each of these provincial territories have a function in your overall kingdom. And if any of them are not functioning on behalf of the kingdom, they will be rogue and will be a hindrance to the total kingdom structure and plan. This is the reason why a Christian can be saved, yet can be struggling in one or more areas of their lives. Many faith filled Christians are always broke, sick, have a bad marriage, have no educational acceleration, or have no social skills. Sometimes a Christian suffers under a mixture of multiple territories which are rogue and not being changed by God's Kingdom and His living Word.

A kingdom or nation must be united under a constitution, the rule of law, and a clear cut code of guidance if that kingdom is to survive and prosper. God's kingdom works within the Holy Bible which is His rule of law, His legal binding document, and the code of guidance for all territories and subjects within that kingdom. It's with this understanding that you are reading God's Word every day and filtering your life's goals, visions and dreams through the Holy Bible.

A person must drag all eight provincial territories of life under the dominion of God's Kingdom. These territories must be affected and changed by God's living Word and His Kingdom plan. When these eight territories begin to move together under God's direction, provision, guidance and vision, a miracle begins to take place. The "whole man" begins to arise and God's miraculous blessings begin to change every area of life for the good.

God wants a person to be balanced. But it's not possible to be balanced and blessed in God's Kingdom if part of your life territory is serving God and other parts are serving their own interests as rogue territories.

Mark 3:24-25 (NIV) If a kingdom is divided against itself, that kingdom cannot stand. If a house is divided against itself, that house cannot stand.

Being double minded is simply having rogue opinions in your life that don't have the same interests as God's Kingdom.

James 1:5-8 (NIV) But when he asks, he must believe and not doubt, because he who doubts is like a wave of the sea, blown and tossed by the wind. That man should not think he will receive anything from the Lord; he is a double-minded man, unstable in all he does.

Bring your whole man under God's Kingdom rule. He has given you dominion authority. Seize these eight provinces of your life and make them subservient to God's Kingdom. How will you do it?

This manual identifies eight provincial areas of your life which you will begin to journal in daily. Each day as you read the Holy Bible, you will begin to get insight and input for your eight provinces. While reading in the Old Testament, an idea or inspiration may come to you concerning your physical body, the need for exercise, eating correctly, or something specific that will help you reach a specific physical goal. A little later, you may get a scriptural inspiration concerning marriage or your finances. Each time you receive inspiration or you believe that God is speaking to you, it's important to go to that section of this manual and journal, log it, and write down what you believe God is saying to you. As you proceed through your first year of reading the Holy Bible, you will begin to develop a divinely inspired understanding and opinion of each of these provinces of life.

At the beginning of a believers life, that person may not have a clue what God wants them to do with their physical, mental, spiritual, social, educational, vocational, financial, or marital life. However, once a believer starts receiving inspiration from the Word of God, and he journals or writes down that inspiration, an opinion begins to be formed about those subjects. This opinion will help you to develop goals for the eight provinces of your life.

At the beginning of each province section is a page for you to write your goals for life. You are encouraged to write down as many goals as you can honestly think of. Then as time passes and you read the Word of God, allow those goals to be manipulated, re-directed and changed by the Holy Spirit as He inspires you each day through the Word of God. At the end of your first year, you should be able to write a solid set of goals for each of your life provinces. With a written vision in place for the eight provinces, your kingdom domain will begin to function and operate in one accord with God's will, and balance will come. Heaven's miraculous interventions will also come to your life and your various provinces. It will be absolutely amazing, and I am positive that you will never desire to leave this form of governing over your provinces and domain. God's Kingdom will literally reign over your kingdom, and you will be successful in bringing all of the provinces of your domain under His kingdom rule.

Rev 11:15 (KJV) . . . and there were great voices in heaven, saying, The kingdoms of this world are become the kingdoms of our Lord, and of his Christ; and he shall reign for ever and ever.

If He is the King and you are His son, then you are also a king in training. The earth and everything in it belongs to the Lord. He is raising up kings and lords from within His household. A king always has a domain to preside over. If you are a king, then you have a domain. And if you have a domain, it's your job to bring that domain under the rule and authority of God's kingdom. And if you are successful, God will give you authority over much more.

Matt 25:21 (NIV) "His master replied, 'Well done, good and faithful servant! You have been faithful with a few things; I will put you in charge of many things. Come and share your master's happiness!'

Seminar Notes For Chapter 7:

Habakkuk 2:2 "Write the vision, and make it plain upon tables, that he may run that readeth it."

Chapter 8
Journaling, Communicating, And Developing Your Life Goals

1. You are going to start by writing your short, medium and long term goals and plans in the eight territorial sections at the back of this workbook. Don't worry, these plans will change and be re-directed as you continue to study them, read the Holy Bible daily, and journal through the year. But write down what you think, believe, and feel at this time. Do your best and ask God for help if you are drawing a blank. Utilize the "keywords" provided in each section of your territory goals (chapters 11 – 18) to help you project and think forward. Remember that thinking forward is a discipline that is learned. If you've never been trained to think forward or vision cast, this is something that you will begin to learn and perfect over the next year.

Prov 16:9 (NIV) In his heart a man plans his course, but the LORD determines his steps.

2. You have committed to read the Holy Bible every day, at the beginning of your day in a quiet, peaceful place where you can filter, focus, and comprehend. Use a version of the bible that you can understand. Some people like the New International Version (NIV), and others like the Living Bible, King James, New King James, etc. Ask your pastor which version is recommended if you don't have a favorite version. You are not required to stop and do an in depth Bible study or a Hebrew word study during your daily goal of reading two Old Testament chapters, two New Testament chapters, five Psalms and one Proverb. Your goal is only to read the material slow enough to comprehend it.

3. While reading the Bible, it is recommended that you develop a relationship of prayer, talking to God, and asking Him questions. Speak softly to the Holy Spirit and ask Him to illuminate the scriptures that you will need for leading the eight provinces of your life each day. Honor and respect the inspiration which will come, along with the thoughts, ideas and visions that you may receive while reading the living, eternal Word of God. You will want to write these inspirations down in the various eight provincial areas of this workbook when you receive them. Make a habit of writing the inspiration immediately when you get it. Habakkuk 2:2 says to write the revelation down and make it plain. This communication between you and God's Holy Spirit will be personal, powerful and life changing. Develop it each day as you let God speak to you through His Word and through the inspiration that comes when you read the Holy Bible.

4. At least once per week, go through any goals that you have set for your life and pray over them. Focus on them and ask God to bless them, direct them, and take control of them. If you sense an inner inspiration to change the goal, modify it or re-direct it, make note of it and write it down. God is helping you to focus your goals and plans as His Word inspires you each day.

Prov 16:2-3 (NIV) All a man's ways seem innocent to him, but motives are weighed by the LORD. Commit to the LORD whatever you do, and your plans will succeed.

Prov 19:21 (NIV) Many are the plans in a man's heart, but it is the LORD's purpose that prevails.

5. As you proceed forward with reading the Bible each day, you are going to experience miraculous things in your life. Be sure to write down these events that occur in this workbook,

and be sure to give God thanks for His blessing upon your life. Share these blessings with others and tell them how God's Word is changing your life each day. Your testimony of God's goodness will be an inspiration to many around you.

6. Make copies of your daily meditation and goal page in chapter 21, and write your goals for the day, as well as a daily meditation scripture that meant something to you during your "5 O'clock Club" reading time.

7. At the end of your one year commitment, re-write your short, medium, and long term goals on paper and keep that paper in front of you always. Pray over these goals every day and ask God to bless them. It is recommended that you start reading the Holy Bible the same way that you started in year one. Get a new Compass Guide manual and keep writing, journaling, and notating the inspiration that you are receiving from the living Word of God. Make notes of the miraculous blessings of God which will overtake your life, so that you can share your life progress with others for years to come.

8. Teach this to your family members, in your church, during business meetings and everywhere you go to help others to realize their full potential and find their true identity and purpose in life.

9. Join the online community at www.doctordanieldaves.com , receive and post daily inspiration with others in the Compass Guide forum.

10. As a final note, Keep this workbook for your children and grand children. This workbook will be a powerful blessing to your family members in the future. They will be able to read it and see how God was speaking to you, and how He guided and blessed you in your life's journey. What a wonderful piece of inheritance to leave to your children and grand children, who will want to know the deep inner workings of the Holy Spirit in your life.

God bless you in this year's upcoming walk with Him as you consume His living, powerful, and eternal Word!

Matt 4:4 (NIV) Jesus answered, "It is written: 'Man does not live on bread alone, but on every word that comes from the mouth of God.' "

Seminar Notes For Chapter 8:

_____

_____

_____

_____

_____

_____

Habakkuk 2:2 "Write the vision, and make it plain upon tables, that he may run that readeth it."

Chapter 9
Creating A Twenty Five Word "Core Life Purpose" Statement

You have learned how to bring eight territories of your life under a unified dominion of God. It's possible that you could become overwhelmed with the complexities of developing a three dimensional, multiple point time line for so many areas of your life. While many people have been taught to focus on one thing their entire lives, you are beginning a training lifestyle that focuses your efforts on multiple times and dimensions, to bring you to a SINGLE focus in life. While some feel overwhelmed at first, I assure you that God has given you the capacity to function within these multiple dimensions and timelines.

Jesus moved in multiple timelines. While He lived in the present, He roamed the halls of the past and He spoke of the future like it was now. While on earth, He lived under an authority that you also live in, which allowed Him to live past, present and future.

Jesus acknowledged that "I Am" before Abraham was born, putting himself presently and historically as the great "I Am" before Abraham was born. This is an amazing truth once a person grasps it.

John 8:57-59 (NIV) "You are not yet fifty years old," the Jews said to him, "and you have seen Abraham!" "I tell you the truth," Jesus answered, "before Abraham was born, I am!" At this, they picked up stones to stone him, but Jesus hid himself, slipping away from the temple grounds.

Jesus commands His disciples to receive the Holy Spirit. Yet, the Holy Spirit will not be given until after His death, burial and resurrection on the day of Pentecost. He also tells His disciples that they have power to forgive sins, but He has not Himself died on the cross for the forgiveness of mankind's sins yet. Jesus is clearly living in the present/future, living in the Spirit which moves backward and forward on the 3rd dimensional human timeline of earthly reality.

John 20:21-23 (NIV) Again Jesus said, "Peace be with you! As the Father has sent me, I am sending you." And with that he breathed on them and said, "Receive the Holy Spirit. If you forgive anyone his sins, they are forgiven; if you do not forgive them, they are not forgiven."

If Jesus was able to move into multiple dimensions of time, then you have the same capacity to do this "In Christ". Therefore, you can be taken into your past by the Holy Sprit or into your future by that same Spirit to be shown the future. You can learn to move in the gifts of the Holy Spirit which include the word of knowledge, word of wisdom, and the gift of prophecy. These are biblical gifts from God which show you the future and what is to come.

*1 Cor 12:4-11 (KJV) Now there are diversities of gifts, but the same Spirit. And there are differences of administrations, but the same Lord. And there are diversities of operations, but it is the same God which worketh all in all. But the manifestation of the Spirit is given to every man to profit withal. For to one is given by the Spirit **the word of wisdom**; to another **the word of knowledge** by the same Spirit; faith by the same Spirit; to another the gifts of healing by the* *same Spirit; the working of miracles; to another **prophecy**; to another discerning of spirits; to another divers kinds of tongues; to another the interpretation of tongues: But all these worketh that one and the selfsame Spirit, dividing to every man severally as he will.*

The Holy Spirit will help you to look into the future and see God's will and thoughts for your life. These are gifts that come from Heaven upon God's sons and daughters who are willing to walk like Jesus, and in fellowship with the Holy Spirit.

God created Adam to work, tend, and manage the garden of Eden. He needed to move in multiple dimensions and multiple timelines. He had to tend, keep and dress the garden. He had dominion over the fish, birds, animals and vegetation. The ground needed to be worked. The serpent needed to be tracked and removed from the garden. Adam would walk with God and name the animals. He would decree things on the earth and those things would stand. To this day, there are animals, birds and earthly things that Adam managed on the earth, which are still in place today.

Gen 1:27-28 (KJV) So God created man in his own image, in the image of God created he him; male and female created he them. And God blessed them, and God said unto them, Be fruitful, and multiply, and replenish the earth, and subdue it: and have dominion over the fish of the sea, and over the fowl of the air, and over every living thing that moveth upon the earth.

If God created Adam and gave him a garden to manage, then indeed God has created you and given you a garden to manage as well. Your garden, kingdom, domain, and territories must come under your management anointing. It's important to know that God wants you to manage multiple dimensions and timelines in your life, and He will give you the wisdom to do it successfully. He will never give you a job to do without giving you the capacity and gifting to handle that job.

Reading Gods Word, praying, journaling, and writing down your goals will help you develop the management anointing so your eight kingdom/garden territories will move together towards one focused CORE THEME.

You will need to create a focused "Core Life Purpose" statement which all eight territories can move towards. This "Core Life Purpose" theme will become your life banner, the point that every area of your life rallies around, and your final life focus. You will write a twenty five word "Core Life Purpose" statement which says it all. This statement sums it up. It tells the whole story. It leaves no stone unturned. The twenty five words in this Core Life Purpose statement will be chosen carefully.

Once you have finished your twenty five word "Core Life Purpose" statement, all eight territories will rally around it. Everything will miraculously come into line and identify with your core purpose. Each part of your life will begin to find it's place in helping to fulfill this "Core Life Purpose".

The kingdom was being handed to David in I Chronicles 12:22. Men and armies began to assemble around David to help him turn the kingdom of Saul over into his hands. These different men and armies had individual strengths and purposes. But they all came to use their strengths in a unified, focused, single effort to turn the kingdom of Saul to David according to the word of the Lord.

1 Chron 12:23 (KJV) And these are the numbers of the bands that were ready armed to the war, and came to David to Hebron, to turn the kingdom of Saul to him, according to the word of the LORD

Your "Core Life Purpose" will be equal to David. It is the "Word of the Lord" for your life. When this twenty five word statement is created and revealed correctly on paper, all eight of your kingdom life provinces will unite, submit, rally, and pledge to help establish this purpose. It will be a unifying and rallying point that will empower you like nothing you've ever experienced!

Hab 2:2-3 (NIV) Then the LORD replied: "Write down the revelation and make it plain on tablets so that a herald may run with it. ³ For the revelation awaits an appointed time; it speaks of the end and will not prove false. Though it linger, wait for it; it will certainly come and will not delay.

Writing your focused "Core Life Purpose" statement will take some time, patience, and developed skill. More than likely, you will take notes, write, and then re-write your statement over and over again, until it fits perfectly. Let's get started.

The first thing you are going to do is to write as many key words as possible that define who you are and what you do (next page). You want to write at least twenty key words. Write more if you possibly can. These key words will be very important because they are going to define the real you. These words will be very important in telling the core life story. Make sure that you are using words that speak loudly about who you are and what you love to do.

On the lines below, write your as many key words that define you, based on the following:
1. Look at your eight territory goals and find key words that represent you from those goals. Also, look at the goal setting key words that are mentioned at the beginning of each territorial goal page.
2. Consider the meaning of your name and see if there are any key words in your name that define who you are. Write them down. For instance, the name "Daniel" means judged of God, and judge of God. These key words may strike an idea for your twenty five word statement. If you don't know how to look up a name, go to www.behindthename.com or any other online name identification site, and check out your name there.
3. Consider your family traits, strengths, callings or purposes. It's possible that you have some of the same qualities and character traits as your parents or other family members. If you can find key words in this area, write them down.
4. Have you had any prophecies or powerful statements made about you in the past which you can relate to? If there are any key words that you can find from those statements, write them down. One young man has always held on to a statement made about him years ago, and his key words are "world changer". Maybe you have a prophecy that is meaningful to you too?

Write down any and all key words you can think of. Try to write at least 20 words, hopefully more.

EXAMPLE: James has written the following key words: Media, Computers, Video, Audio, Songwriting, Singing And Worship, Guitar, Piano, Missions, Travel, Evangelism, Team Leadership, Business, Wealth, Giving, Feeding Children,

Your Key Words For Your "Core Life Purpose" Statement:

Now that you have written numerous keywords that help to identify who you are at your core, you are going to begin writing a twenty five word statement which best represents you at your core. This core statement will come from your heart. It will be a purpose statement that comes up from your inner core and expresses itself on paper. You will choose your words wisely. Each word is very important. Once you write your first draft, you will look it over and plan to re-write it. Many words that you used in the first draft can probably be eliminated or merged. The more words you can merge or eliminate, the more clearly you can build your twenty five word statement.

EXAMPLE: James wrote his first draft of his Core Life Purpose statement like this:

DRAFT #1: To use my God given video and audio talents to reach the world for Jesus. To be a worship leader and missionary in the church.

Draft #1: Your "Core Life Statement" In 25 Words

In the example, James had trouble getting all of his vision into his twenty five word statement. He left out "Team Leadership, Business, Wealth, Giving and Feeding Children. These are very important parts of his core life purpose, but they are not in the draft version of his statement. Therefore, we are going to make some changes to his first draft, and we are going to change some words. The end result will be a refined statement that makes total sense to James, and which tells the whole story.

DRAFT #1: To use my God given video and audio talents to reach the world for Jesus. To be a worship leader and missionary in the church.

First of all, we know that James is gifted and talented, and that God has given these talents to him. Therefore, we can drop the following words off of the statement, because they're already self evident:

DRAFT #1: ~~To use my God given video and audio talents~~ *to reach the world for Jesus. To be a worship leader and missionary in the church.*

Written differently:

DRAFT #2: Using media to reach the world for Jesus. To be a worship leader and missionary in the church.

Now we know that James will use his worship leadership and missionary work in and for the church. And we also know that we have not yet used the words "Team Leadership, Business, Wealth, Giving, Feeding Children" in the core purpose statement. It's possible that we can merge some words and ideas to get these important core concepts into his statement. James re-writes his draft statement over and over, counting the words to make sure that he has exactly twenty five words. He ends up with draft #3 which says:

DRAFT #3: Using media, church worship and leading missions teams to reach the world for Jesus. Use business wealth creation to feed hungry children around the world.

James now has modified his twenty five word core purpose statement and he feels really good about it. This statement is written from his heart, and now he has it on paper, in front of him, and available for the world to see. It says:

FINAL TWENTY FIVE WORD STATEMENT: Using media, church worship and lead missions teams to reach the world for Jesus. Use business wealth creation to feed hungry children around the world.

NOTE: James may want to continue refining his twenty five word statement in the future. The last three words of his statement say "around the world". However, he could replace these three words with the word "internationally" or "worldwide". This would give him two more powerful key words to use in his twenty five word statement to help expose his core purpose on paper.

Many people are elated and filled with joy, emotion, and deep satisfaction when they see this finished twenty five word core statement in front of them.

Now, look at your twenty five word statement and try to re-write it. Merge words to make the statement stronger. Delete extra words that don't really help the statement. We already know that you love God, and that you are doing His will. Empower your twenty five words by making each of them count.

Draft #2: Your "Core Life Statement" In 25 Words

Draft #3: Your "Core Life Statement" In 25 Words

FINAL TWENTY FIVE WORD CORE LIFE STATEMENT:

_____
_____
_____

Re-write this statement as many times as needed until you feel really good about this statement. You will know when you are finished with it because this statement will jump off of the pages of this workbook and it will be YOU ON PAPER! You will know it.

NOTE #1: You may need to take some time with this. One out of four people need to focus, pray, and take a couple of days with this final statement. But it's important that you break through and get the statement accomplished. This is a KEY to your success. Therefore, take the time necessary, fast if necessary, and don't leave the table until you have this statement completed to your inner satisfaction. You are breaking through into an area that you've never been before. You are digging up the deep purposes of your heart and writing them on paper. Some people are very complex and their callings are very detailed. And some things which need to be written down on paper have never been discussed or brought up from your heart before. Get your breakthrough. Stick with this until you are satisfied with your final statement.

NOTE #2: Once you have a good statement that you are confident in, remember that this statement will need to pass through the mind of God and through the fire of His Word. Therefore, you may find yourself modifying it further in the coming weeks or months. This is absolutely normal and expected of anyone who has chosen to bring God into their goal setting and life plan. Be flexible and willing to change or modify this twenty five word statement in the coming weeks or months.

With your Twenty Five Word Core Life Statement in place, now your eight kingdom life territories have a rallying point and a focused statement that they can relate to. While each of your kingdom territories has it's own identity, it's important that all eight work together to fulfill a central theme, a central focus, and a central "core" purpose in life. With this core statement in place, all eight territories will unify and become one to push this purpose forward into complete fulfillment.

Copy this statement on paper. Write it in Chapter 20 and on note cards. Paste it on your refrigerator. Put it on the dashboard of your car. Tape it to your computer monitor screen. Then live it. Give quality time to it. Memorize it and activate it in all eight territories of your life. Commit to doing at least one thing per day to reach forward and fulfill your core statement and territorial goals. Congratulations!

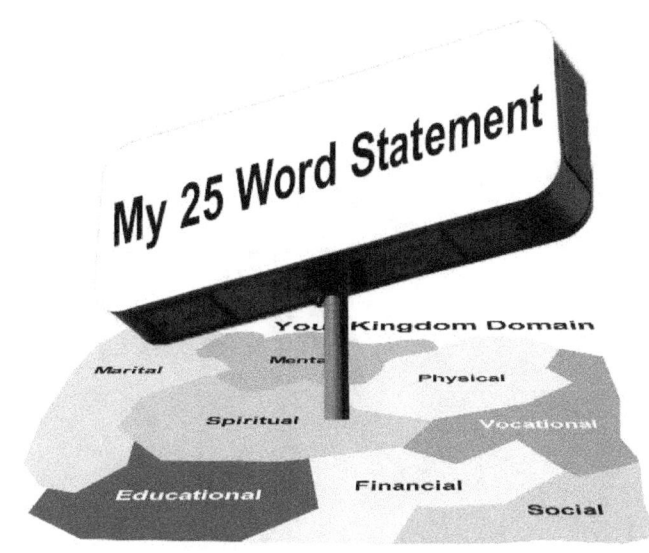

44

Chapter 10
Final Instructions For The Best Use Of This Workbook

You have learned that God has a divine plan mapped out for you. However, that plan is hidden deep down inside of your heart. It's your job to dig down deep and retrieve the plan, filtering it through prayer and reading of God's Word every day. You will learn to work together with the Holy Spirit to negotiate the plan according to His will and purpose. Then you will begin to focus, writing the vision down in this workbook, and then will walk it and work it out on a daily basis so that you can see it come to pass in your lifetime. You will focus, pray, and move in multiple dimensions of time including one year, five years, ten years, twenty years and fifty years into the future.

1. Start by writing down your short, medium, and long term goals for each territory of your life (eight total – physical, mental, spiritual, social, educational, vocational, marital and financial). You will find the "Goals" page at the front of each territory section in this workbook. Take your time and quietly meditate on your future, asking God to help you with inspirational thoughts and Holy Spirit inspired vision. Use the "Key Words" at the beginning of each territorial section to help stimulate your thinking.

2. Make the supreme one year commitment of reading the Word of God every day for one year and sign the agreement with God in Chapter six. This will serve as your filter, the heavenly fire, and the cleansing water which will purify your life, goals, and vision. Daily interaction with the Word will become a lamp for your feet and a light to your path (Psalm 119:105) and the Holy Spirit will use the Holy Bible to inspire you, motivate, and speak to you clearly about your life's goals and divine purpose on earth.

3. Write your twenty five word "Core Life Statement" (chapter nine) so that you have a solid understanding of who you are in twenty five words.

4. You will journal in this workbook each day as you read the Word of God. When you find a scripture that fits one or more of your eight "life territories", journal that scripture and what it means to you in your notes. If God is speaking to you, teaching you, or inspiring you, write it down so you can remember it. If you need to modify or change one of your goals because of this fresh direction from God's Word, then do it. Make note of every meeting that you have with God's Word and the Holy Spirit when He is directing or changing your direction. Don't worry. An eraser will absolutely be needed, because you're going to be making many changes and additions to your goals as the Word of God filters through you each day.

5. Pick a day each week and go back over your goals. A great day is early Sunday morning before church services. Arm yourself with your goals and visions, and then let the Sunday morning church message inspire you. Pray over your goals. Ask God to filter and focus them through His Word each day that you read. Ask for Holy Spirit inspiration to help you understand your goals and to write the vision correctly. Ask God to help you fulfill your goals and visions. Thank Him for helping you draw near to Him and for His help with your life's goals and vision.

6. At the end of one year, you will re-write your short, medium, and long term goals. Check off any goals that were reached during your filter and focus year. Notice the difference in your goals and vision from the beginning of the year to the end of the year. Your goals have been modified, changed, advanced, cleansed, and purified by the Holy Spirit and the powerful Word of God. Congratulations! You now have a complete set of short, medium and long term goals which have been filtered through the entire Holy Bible and bathed in one solid year of prayer, filtering, and focus. You can be sure that God is leading you towards these goals and visions for your life, and you will have found that He is getting involved with you to help you complete the tasks and fulfill the goals. Your acquired discipline is setting the course for the rest of your life.

7. Start the process over again each year. Continually add short term goals which will help you to reach your medium and long term goals. Keep reading God's Word and asking the Holy Spirit for insight and understanding, for open doors and miracles to help accomplish your goals. They are most certainly goals that God wants you to pursue because they have been brought to the surface from deep in your heart. They have ran through the cleansing, purifying Word of God and prayer, and they survived the heat and fire of the Holy Spirit. They are gold, silver and precious stones for you to honor, pursue and possess. Congratulations!

Seminar Notes For Chapter 10:

Habakkuk 2:2 "Write the vision, and make it plain upon tables, that he may run that readeth it."

Chapter 11: "The Five O'clock Club"
Daily Bible Reading Calendar

Read 2 Chapters In The Old Testament, Two Chapters In The New Testament, Five Chapters In Psalms, One Chapter In Proverbs. When you have finished reading for that day, put a check on the right hand box. If you ever fall behind, make up the reading the next day and fill in the check mark for each day. Make sure to add a journal entry of some kind each day that you read the bible. Pray and ask God to speak into your life from His living Word. It's recommended that you start reading at the current date on this calendar. You will be joining many believers from around the world who are also reading the same scriptures that day. Go to www.doctordanieldaves.com, join the Compass Guide forum, read and post comments regarding the day's scriptural reading adventure.

1-Jan	Genesis 1-2	Matthew 1-2	Psalms 1-5	Proverbs 1	
2-Jan	Genesis 3-4	Matthew 3-4	Psalms 6-10	Proverbs 2	
3-Jan	Genesis 5-6	Matthew 5-6	Psalms 11-15	Proverbs 3	
4-Jan	Genesis 7-8	Matthew 7-8	Psalms 16-20	Proverbs 4	
5-Jan	Genesis 9-10	Matthew 9-10	Psalms 21-25	Proverbs 5	
6-Jan	Genesis 11-12	Matthew 11-12	Psalms 26-30	Proverbs 6	
7-Jan	Genesis 13-14	Matthew 13-14	Psalms 31-35	Proverbs 7	
8-Jan	Genesis 15-16	Matthew 15-16	Psalms 36-40	Proverbs 8	
9-Jan	Genesis 17-18	Matthew 17-18	Psalms 41-45	Proverbs 9	
10-Jan	Genesis 19-20	Matthew 19-20	Psalms 46-50	Proverbs 10	
11-Jan	Genesis 21-22	Matthew 21-22	Psalms 51-55	Proverbs 11	
12-Jan	Genesis 23-24	Matthew 23-24	Psalms 56-60	Proverbs 12	
13-Jan	Genesis 25-26	Matthew 25-26	Psalms 61-65	Proverbs 13	
14-Jan	Genesis 27-28	Matthew 27-28	Psalms 66-70	Proverbs 14	
15-Jan	Genesis 29-30	Mark 1-2	Psalms 71-75	Proverbs 15	
16-Jan	Genesis 31-32	Mark 3-4	Psalms 76-80	Proverbs 16	
17-Jan	Genesis 33-34	Mark 5-6	Psalms 81-85	Proverbs 17	
18-Jan	Genesis 35-36	Mark 7-8	Psalms 86-90	Proverbs 18	
19-Jan	Genesis 37-38	Mark 9-10	Psalms 91-95	Proverbs 19	
20-Jan	Genesis 39-40	Mark 11-12	Psalms 96-100	Proverbs 20	
21-Jan	Genesis 41-42	Mark 13-14	Psalms 101-105	Proverbs 21	
22-Jan	Genesis 43-44	Mark 15-16	Psalms 106-110	Proverbs 22	
23-Jan	Genesis 45-47	Luke 1-2	Psalms 111-115	Proverbs 23	
24-Jan	Genesis 48 - 50	Luke 3-4	Psalms 116-120	Proverbs 24	
25-Jan	Exodus 1-2	Luke 5-6	Psalms 121-125	Proverbs 25	
26-Jan	Exodus 3-4	Luke 7-8	Psalms 126-130	Proverbs 26	
27-Jan	Exodus 5-6	Luke 9-10	Psalms 131-135	Proverbs 27	
28-Jan	Exodus 7-8	Luke 11-12	Psalms 136-140	Proverbs 28	
29-Jan	Exodus 9-10	Luke 13-14	Psalms 141-145	Proverbs 29	
30-Jan	Exodus 11-12	Luke 15-16	Psalms 146-150	Proverbs 30	

"The Five O'clock Club" Daily Bible Reading Calendar

31-Jan	Exodus 13-14	Luke 17-18	Psalms 1-5	Proverbs 31	
1-Feb	Exodus 15-16	Luke 19-20	Psalms 6-10	Proverbs 1	
2-Feb	Exodus 17-18	Luke 21-22	Psalms 11-15	Proverbs 2	
3-Feb	Exodus 19-20	Luke 23-24	Psalms 16-20	Proverbs 3	
4-Feb	Exodus 21-22	John 1-2	Psalms 21-25	Proverbs 4	
5-Feb	Exodus 23-24	John 3-4	Psalms 26-30	Proverbs 5	
6-Feb	Exodus 25-26	John 5-6	Psalms 31-35	Proverbs 6	
7-Feb	Exodus 27-28	John 7-8	Psalms 36-40	Proverbs 7	
8-Feb	Exodus 29-30	John 9-10	Psalms 41-45	Proverbs 8	
9-Feb	Exodus 31-32	John 11-12	Psalms 46-50	Proverbs 9	
10-Feb	Exodus 33-34	John 13-14	Psalms 51-55	Proverbs 10	
11-Feb	Exodus 35-37	John 15-16	Psalms 56-60	Proverbs 11	
12-Feb	Exodus 38-40	John 17-18	Psalms 61-65	Proverbs 12	
13-Feb	Leviticus 1-2	John 19-20	Psalms 66-70	Proverbs 13	
14-Feb	Leviticus 3-4	John 21	Psalms 71-75	Proverbs 14	
15-Feb	Leviticus 5-6	Acts 1-2	Psalms 76-80	Proverbs 15	
16-Feb	Leviticus 7-8	Acts 3-4	Psalms 81-85	Proverbs 16	
17-Feb	Leviticus 9-10	Acts 5-6	Psalms 86-90	Proverbs 17	
18-Feb	Leviticus 11-12	Acts 7-8	Psalms 91-95	Proverbs 18	
19-Feb	Leviticus 13-14	Acts 9-10	Psalms 96-100	Proverbs 19	
20-Feb	Leviticus 15-16	Acts 11-12	Psalms 101-105	Proverbs 20	
21-Feb	Leviticus 17-18	Acts 13-14	Psalms 106-110	Proverbs 21	
22-Feb	Leviticus 19-20	Acts 15-16	Psalms 111-115	Proverbs 22	
23-Feb	Leviticus 21-22	Acts 17-18	Psalms 116-120	Proverbs 23	
24-Feb	Leviticus 23-24	Acts 19-20	Psalms 121-125	Proverbs 24	
25-Feb	Leviticus 25-27	Acts 21-22	Psalms 126-130	Proverbs 25	
26-Feb	Numbers 1-2	Acts 23-24	Psalms 131-135	Proverbs 26	
27-Feb	Numbers 3-4	Acts 25-26	Psalms 136-140	Proverbs 27	
28-Feb	Numbers 5-6	Acts 27-28	Psalms 141-145	Proverbs 28	
29-Feb	Day Off	Day Off	Day Off	Proverbs 29	
1-Mar	Numbers 7-8	Romans 1-2	Psalms 146-150	Proverbs 1	
2-Mar	Numbers 9-10	Romans 3-4	Psalms 1-5	Proverbs 2	
3-Mar	Numbers 11-12	Romans 5-6	Psalms 6-10	Proverbs 3	
4-Mar	Numbers 13-14	Romans 7-8	Psalms 11-15	Proverbs 4	
5-Mar	Numbers 15-16	Romans 9-10	Psalms 16-20	Proverbs 5	
6-Mar	Numbers 17-18	Romans 11-12	Psalms 21-25	Proverbs 6	
7-Mar	Numbers 19-20	Romans 13-14	Psalms 26-30	Proverbs 7	

"The Five O'clock Club"
Daily Bible Reading Calendar

8-Mar	Numbers 21-22	Romans 15-16	Psalms 31-35	Proverbs 8
9-Mar	Numbers 23-24	1 Cor. 1-2	Psalms 36-40	Proverbs 9
10-Mar	Numbers 25-26	1 Cor. 3-4	Psalms 41-45	Proverbs 10
11-Mar	Numbers 27-28	1 Cor. 5-6	Psalms 46-50	Proverbs 11
12-Mar	Numbers 29-30	1 Cor. 7-8	Psalms 51-55	Proverbs 12
13-Mar	Numbers 31-33	1 Cor. 9-10	Psalms 56-60	Proverbs 13
14-Mar	Numbers 34-36	1 Cor. 11-12	Psalms 61-65	Proverbs 14
15-Mar	Deut. 1-2	1 Cor. 13-14	Psalms 66-70	Proverbs 15
16-Mar	Deut. 3-4	1 Cor. 15-16	Psalms 71-75	Proverbs 16
17-Mar	Deut. 5-6	2 Cor 1-2	Psalms 76-80	Proverbs 17
18-Mar	Deut. 7-8	2 Cor. 3-4	Psalms 81-85	Proverbs 18
19-Mar	Deut 9-10	2 Cor. 5-6	Psalms 86-90	Proverbs 19
20-Mar	Deut 11-12	2 Cor. 7-8	Psalms 91-95	Proverbs 20
21-Mar	Deut 13-14	2 Cor. 9-10	Psalms 96-100	Proverbs 21
22-Mar	Deut 15-16	2 Cor. 11-12	Psalms 101-105	Proverbs 22
23-Mar	Deut 17-18	2 Cor. 13	Psalms 106-110	Proverbs 23
24-Mar	Deut 19-20	Galatians 1-2	Psalms 111-115	Proverbs 24
25-Mar	Deut 21-22	Galatians 3-4	Psalms 116-120	Proverbs 25
26-Mar	Deut 23-24	Galatians 5-6	Psalms 121-125	Proverbs 26
27-Mar	Deut 25-26	Ephesians 1-2	Psalms 126-130	Proverbs 27
28-Mar	Deut. 27-28	Ephesians 3-4	Psalms 131-135	Proverbs 28
29-Mar	Deut. 29-31	Ephesians 5-6	Psalms 136-140	Proverbs 29
30-Mar	Deut. 32-34	Philippians 1-2	Psalms 141-145	Proverbs 30
31-Mar	Joshua 1-2	Philippians 3-4	Psalms 146-150	Proverbs 31
1-Apr	Joshua 3-4	Colossians 1-2	Psalms 1-5	Proverbs 1
2-Apr	Joshua 5-6	Colossians 3-4	Psalms 6-10	Proverbs 2
3-Apr	Joshua 7-8	1 Thess. 1-2	Psalms 11-15	Proverbs 3
4-Apr	Joshua 9-10	1 Thess. 3-4	Psalms 16-20	Proverbs 4
5-Apr	Joshua 11-12	1 Thess. 5	Psalms 21-25	Proverbs 5
6-Apr	Joshua 13-14	2 Thess. 1-2	Psalms 26-30	Proverbs 6
7-Apr	Joshua 15-16	2 Thess. 3	Psalms 31-35	Proverbs 7
8-Apr	Joshua 17-18	1 Tim. 1-2	Psalms 36-40	Proverbs 8
9-Apr	Joshua 19-21	1 Tim. 3-4	Psalms 41-45	Proverbs 9
10-Apr	Joshua 22-24	1 Tim. 5-6	Psalms 46-50	Proverbs 10
11-Apr	Judges 1-2	2 Tim. 1-2	Psalms 51-55	Proverbs 11
12-Apr	Judges 3-4	2 Tim. 3-4	Psalms 56-60	Proverbs 12
13-Apr	Judges 5-6	Titus 1-2	Psalms 61-65	Proverbs 13

"The Five O'clock Club"
Daily Bible Reading Calendar

14-Apr	Judges 7-8	Titus 3, Philem. 1	Psalms 66-70	Proverbs 14
15-Apr	Judges 9-10	Hebrews 1-2	Psalms 71-75	Proverbs 15
16-Apr	Judges 11-12	Hebrews 3-4	Psalms 76-80	Proverbs 16
17-Apr	Judges 13-14	Hebrews 5-6	Psalms 81-85	Proverbs 17
18-Apr	Judges 15-16	Hebrews 7-8	Psalms 86-90	Proverbs 18
19-Apr	Judges 17-18	Hebrews 9-10	Psalms 91-95	Proverbs 19
20-Apr	Judges 19-21	Hebrews 11-12	Psalms 96-100	Proverbs 20
21-Apr	Ruth 1-2	Hebrews 13	Psalms 101-105	Proverbs 21
22-Apr	Ruth 3-4	James 1-2	Psalms 106-110	Proverbs 22
23-Apr	1 Sam. 1-2	James 3-4	Psalms 111-115	Proverbs 23
24-Apr	1 Sam. 3-4	James 5	Psalms 116-120	Proverbs 24
25-Apr	1 Sam. 5-6	1 Peter 1-2	Psalms 121-125	Proverbs 25
26-Apr	1 Sam. 7-8	1 Peter 3-4	Psalms 126-130	Proverbs 26
27-Apr	1 Sam. 9-10	1 Peter 5	Psalms 131-135	Proverbs 27
28-Apr	1 Sam. 11-12	2 Peter 1-2	Psalms 136-140	Proverbs 28
29-Apr	1 Sam. 13-14	2 Peter 3	Psalms 141-145	Proverbs 29
30-Apr	1 Sam. 15-16	1 John 1-2	Psalms 146-150	Proverbs 30
1-May	1 Sam. 17-18	1 John 3-4	Psalms 1-5	Proverbs 1
2-May	1 Sam. 19-20	1 Jn. 5, 2 Jn. 1	Psalms 6-10	Proverbs 2
3-May	1 Sam. 21-22	3 John 1	Psalms 11-15	Proverbs 3
4-May	1 Sam. 23-24	Jude	Psalms 16-20	Proverbs 4
5-May	1 Sam. 25-26	Revelations 1-2	Psalms 21-25	Proverbs 5
6-May	1 Sam. 27-28	Revelations 3-4	Psalms 26-30	Proverbs 6
7-May	1 Sam. 29-30	Revelations 5-6	Psalms 31-35	Proverbs 7
8-May	1 Sam. 31	Revelations 7-8	Psalms 36-40	Proverbs 8
9-May	2 Sam. 1-2	Revelations 9-10	Psalms 41-45	Proverbs 9
10-May	2 Sam. 3-4	Rev. 11-12	Psalms 46-50	Proverbs 10
11-May	2 Sam. 5-6	Rev. 13-14	Psalms 51-55	Proverbs 11
12-May	2 Sam. 7-8	Rev. 15-16	Psalms 56-60	Proverbs 12
13-May	2 Sam. 9-10	Rev. 17-18	Psalms 61-65	Proverbs 13
14-May	2 Sam. 11-12	Rev. 19-20	Psalms 66-70	Proverbs 14
15-May	2 Sam. 13-14	Rev. 21-22	Psalms 71-75	Proverbs 15
16-May	2 Sam. 15-16	Matthew 1-2	Psalms 76-80	Proverbs 16
17-May	2 Sam. 17-18	Matthew 3-4	Psalms 81-85	Proverbs 17
18-May	2 Sam. 19-20	Matthew 5-6	Psalms 86-90	Proverbs 18
19-May	2 Sam. 21-22	Matthew 7-8	Psalms 91-95	Proverbs 19
20-May	2 Sam. 23-24	Matthew 9-10	Psalms 96-100	Proverbs 20

"The Five O'clock Club"
Daily Bible Reading Calendar

21-May	1 Kings 1-2	Matthew 11-12	Psalms 101-105	Proverbs 21	
22-May	1 Kings 3-4	Matthew 13-14	Psalms 106-110	Proverbs 22	
23-May	1 Kings 5-6	Matthew 15-16	Psalms 111-115	Proverbs 23	
24-May	1 Kings 7-8	Matthew 17-18	Psalms 116-120	Proverbs 24	
25-May	1 Kings 9-10	Matthew 19-20	Psalms 121-125	Proverbs 25	
26-May	1 Kings 11-12	Matthew 21-22	Psalms 126-130	Proverbs 26	
27-May	1 Kings 13-14	Matthew 23-24	Psalms 131-135	Proverbs 27	
28-May	1 Kings 15-16	Matthew 25-26	Psalms 136-140	Proverbs 28	
29-May	1 Kings 17-18	Matthew 27-28	Psalms 141-145	Proverbs 29	
30-May	1 Kings 19-20	Mark 1-2	Psalms 146-150	Proverbs 30	
31-May	1 Kings 21-22	Mark 3-4	Psalms 1-5	Proverbs 31	
1-Jun	2 Kings 1-2	Mark 5-6	Psalms 6-10	Proverbs 1	
2-Jun	2 Kings 3-4	Mark 7-8	Psalms 11-15	Proverbs 2	
3-Jun	2 Kings 5-6	Mark 9-10	Psalms 16-20	Proverbs 3	
4-Jun	2 Kings 7-8	Mark 11-12	Psalms 21-25	Proverbs 4	
5-Jun	2 Kings 9-10	Mark 13-14	Psalms 26-30	Proverbs 5	
6-Jun	2 Kings 11-12	Mark 15-16	Psalms 31-35	Proverbs 6	
7-Jun	2 Kings 13-14	Luke 1-2	Psalms 36-40	Proverbs 7	
8-Jun	2 Kings 15-16	Luke 3-4	Psalms 41-45	Proverbs 8	
9-Jun	2 Kings 17-18	Luke 5-6	Psalms 46-50	Proverbs 9	
10-Jun	2 Kings 19-20	Luke 7-8	Psalms 51-55	Proverbs 10	
11-Jun	2 Kings 21-22	Luke 9-10	Psalms 56-60	Proverbs 11	
12-Jun	2 Kings 23-25	Luke 11-12	Psalms 61-65	Proverbs 12	
13-Jun	1 Chronicles 1-2	Luke 13-14	Psalms 66-70	Proverbs 13	
14-Jun	1 Chronicles 3-4	Luke 15-16	Psalms 71-75	Proverbs 14	
15-Jun	1 Chronicles 5-6	Luke 17-18	Psalms 76-80	Proverbs 15	
16-Jun	1 Chronicles 7-8	Luke 19-20	Psalms 81-85	Proverbs 16	
17-Jun	1 Chronicles 9-10	Luke 21-22	Psalms 86-90	Proverbs 17	
18-Jun	1 Chron. 11-12	Luke 23-24	Psalms 91-95	Proverbs 18	
19-Jun	1 Chron. 13-14	John 1-2	Psalms 96-100	Proverbs 19	
20-Jun	1 Chron. 15-16	John 3-4	Psalms 101-105	Proverbs 20	
21-Jun	1 Chron. 17-18	John 5-6	Psalms 106-110	Proverbs 21	
22-Jun	1 Chron. 19-20	John 7-8	Psalms 111-115	Proverbs 22	
23-Jun	1 Chron. 21-22	John 9-10	Psalms 116-120	Proverbs 23	
24-Jun	1 Chron. 23-25	John 11-12	Psalms 121-125	Proverbs 24	
25-Jun	1 Chron. 26-29	John 13-14	Psalms 126-130	Proverbs 25	
26-Jun	2 Chronicles 1-2	John 15-16	Psalms 131-135	Proverbs 26	

"The Five O'clock Club"
Daily Bible Reading Calendar

27-Jun	2 Chronicles 3-4	John 17-18	Psalms 136-140	Proverbs 27	
28-Jun	2 Chronicles 5-6	John 19-20	Psalms 141-145	Proverbs 28	
29-Jun	2 Chronicles 7-8	John 21	Psalms 146-150	Proverbs 29	
30-Jun	2 Chronicles 9-10	Acts 1-2	Psalms 1-5	Proverbs 30	
1-Jul	2 Chron. 11-12	Acts 3-4	Psalms 6-10	Proverbs 1	
2-Jul	2 Chron. 13-14	Acts 5-6	Psalms 11-15	Proverbs 2	
3-Jul	2 Chron. 15-16	Acts 7-8	Psalms 16-20	Proverbs 3	
4-Jul	2 Chon. 17-18	Acts 9-10	Psalms 21-25	Proverbs 4	
5-Jul	2 Chron. 19-20	Acts 11-12	Psalms 26-30	Proverbs 5	
6-Jul	2 Chron. 21-22	Acts 13-14	Psalms 31-35	Proverbs 6	
7-Jul	2 Chron. 23-24	Acts 15-16	Psalms 36-40	Proverbs 7	
8-Jul	2 Chron. 25-26	Acts 17-18	Psalms 41-45	Proverbs 8	
9-Jul	2 Chron. 27-28	Acts 19-20	Psalms 46-50	Proverbs 9	
10-Jul	2 Chron. 29-30	Acts 21-22	Psalms 51-55	Proverbs 10	
11-Jul	2 Chron. 31-33	Acts 23-24	Psalms 56-60	Proverbs 11	
12-Jul	2 Chron. 34-36	Acts 25-26	Psalms 61-65	Proverbs 12	
13-Jul	Ezra 1-2	Acts 27-28	Psalms 66-70	Proverbs 13	
14-Jul	Ezra 3-4	Romans 1-2	Psalms 71-75	Proverbs 14	
15-Jul	Ezra 5-6	Romans 3-4	Psalms 76-80	Proverbs 15	
16-Jul	Ezra 7-8	Romans 5-6	Psalms 81-85	Proverbs 16	
17-Jul	Ezra 9-10	Romans 7-8	Psalms 86-90	Proverbs 17	
18-Jul	Neh. 1-2	Romans 9-10	Psalms 91-95	Proverbs 18	
19-Jul	Neh. 3-4	Romans 11-12	Psalms 96-100	Proverbs 19	
20-Jul	Neh. 5-6	Romans 13-14	Psalms 101-105	Proverbs 20	
21-Jul	Neh. 7-8	Romans 15-16	Psalms 106-110	Proverbs 21	
22-Jul	Neh. 9-10	1 Cor. 1-2	Psalms 111-115	Proverbs 22	
23-Jul	Neh. 11-13	1 Cor. 3-4	Psalms 116-120	Proverbs 23	
24-Jul	Esther 1-2	1 Cor. 5-6	Psalms 121-125	Proverbs 24	
25-Jul	Esther 3-4	1 Cor. 7-8	Psalms 126-130	Proverbs 25	
26-Jul	Esther 5-6	1 Cor. 9-10	Psalms 131-135	Proverbs 26	
27-Jul	Esther 7-8	1 Cor. 11-12	Psalms 136-140	Proverbs 27	
28-Jul	Esther 9-10	1 Cor. 13-14	Psalms 141-145	Proverbs 28	
29-Jul	Job 1-2	1 Cor. 15-16	Psalms 146-150	Proverbs 29	
30-Jul	Job 3-4	2 Cor. 1-2	Psalms 1-5	Proverbs 30	
31-Jul	Job 5-6	2 Cor. 3-4	Psalms 6-10	Proverbs 31	
1-Aug	Job 7-8	2 Cor. 5-6	Psalms 11-15	Proverbs 1	
2-Aug	Job 9-10	2 Cor. 7-8	Psalms 16-20	Proverbs 2	

"The Five O'clock Club"
Daily Bible Reading Calendar

3-Aug	Job 11-12	2 Cor. 9-10	Psalms 21-25	Proverbs 3
4-Aug	Job 13-14	2 Cor. 11-12	Psalms 26-30	Proverbs 4
5-Aug	Job 15-16	2 Cor. 13	Psalms 31-35	Proverbs 5
6-Aug	Job 17-18	Galatians 1-2	Psalms 36-40	Proverbs 6
7-Aug	Job 19-20	Galatians 3-4	Psalms 41-45	Proverbs 7
8-Aug	Job 21-22	Galatians 5-6	Psalms 46-50	Proverbs 8
9-Aug	Job 23-24	Ephesians 1-2	Psalms 51-55	Proverbs 9
10-Aug	Job 25-26	Ephesians 3-4	Psalms 56-60	Proverbs 10
11-Aug	Job 27-28	Ephesians 5-6	Psalms 61-65	Proverbs 11
12-Aug	Job 29-30	Philippians 1-2	Psalms 66-70	Proverbs 12
13-Aug	Job 31-32	Philippians 3-4	Psalms 71-75	Proverbs 13
14-Aug	Job 33-34	Colossians 1-2	Psalms 76-80	Proverbs 14
15-Aug	Job 35-36	Colossians 3-4	Psalms 81-85	Proverbs 15
16-Aug	Job 37-38	1 Thess. 1-2	Psalms 86-90	Proverbs 16
17-Aug	Job 39-40	1 Thess. 3-4	Psalms 91-95	Proverbs 17
18-Aug	Job 41-42	1 Thess. 5	Psalms 96-100	Proverbs 18
19-Aug	Ecclesiastes 1-2	2 Thess. 1-2	Psalms 101-105	Proverbs 19
20-Aug	Ecclesiastes 3-4	2 Thess. 3	Psalms 106-110	Proverbs 20
21-Aug	Ecclesiastes 5-6	1 Tim. 1-2	Psalms 111-115	Proverbs 21
22-Aug	Ecclesiastes 7-8	1 Tim. 3-4	Psalms 116-120	Proverbs 22
23-Aug	Ecclesiastes 9-10	1 Tim. 5-6	Psalms 121-125	Proverbs 23
24-Aug	Ecclesiastes 11-12	2 Tim. 1-2	Psalms 126-130	Proverbs 24
25-Aug	Song Of Songs 1-2	2 Tim. 3-4	Psalms 131-135	Proverbs 25
26-Aug	Song Of Songs 3-4	Titus 1-2	Psalms 136-140	Proverbs 26
27-Aug	Song Of Songs 5-6	Titus 3, Philem. 1	Psalms 141-145	Proverbs 27
28-Aug	Song Of Songs 7-8	Hebrews 1-2	Psalms 146-150	Proverbs 28
29-Aug	Isaiah 1-2	Hebrews 3-4	Psalms 1-5	Proverbs 29
30-Aug	Isaiah 3-4	Hebrews 5-6	Psalms 6-10	Proverbs 30
31-Aug	Isaiah 5-6	Hebrews 7-8	Psalms 11-15	Proverbs 31
1-Sep	Isaiah 7-8	Hebrews 9-10	Psalms 16-20	Proverbs 1
2-Sep	Isaiah 9-10	Hebrews 11-12	Psalms 21-25	Proverbs 2
3-Sep	Isaiah 11-12	Hebrews 13	Psalms 26-30	Proverbs 3
4-Sep	Isaiah 13-14	James 1-2	Psalms 31-35	Proverbs 4
5-Sep	Isaiah 15-16	James 3-4	Psalms 36-40	Proverbs 5
6-Sep	Isaiah 17-18	James 5	Psalms 41-45	Proverbs 6
7-Sep	Isaiah 19-20	1 Peter 1-2	Psalms 46-50	Proverbs 7
8-Sep	Isaiah 21-22	1 Peter 3-4	Psalms 51-55	Proverbs 8

"The Five O'clock Club"
Daily Bible Reading Calendar

9-Sep	Isaiah 23-24	1 Peter 5	Psalms 56-60	Proverbs 9
10-Sep	Isaiah 25-26	2 Peter 1-2	Psalms 61-65	Proverbs 10
11-Sep	Isaiah 27-28	2 Peter 3	Psalms 66-70	Proverbs 11
12-Sep	Isaiah 29-30	1 John 1-2	Psalms 71-75	Proverbs 12
13-Sep	Isaiah 31-32	1 John 3-4	Psalms 76-80	Proverbs 13
14-Sep	Isaiah 33-34	1 Jn. 5, 2 Jn. 1	Psalms 81-85	Proverbs 14
15-Sep	Isaiah 35-36	3 John 1	Psalms 86-90	Proverbs 15
16-Sep	Isaiah 37-38	Jude	Psalms 91-95	Proverbs 16
17-Sep	Isaiah 39-40	Revelations 1-2	Psalms 96-100	Proverbs 17
18-Sep	Isaiah 41-42	Revelations 3-4	Psalms 101-105	Proverbs 18
19-Sep	Isaiah 43-44	Revelations 5-6	Psalms 106-110	Proverbs 19
20-Sep	Isaiah 45-46	Revelations 7-8	Psalms 111-115	Proverbs 20
21-Sep	Isaiah 47-48	Revelations 9-10	Psalms 116-120	Proverbs 21
22-Sep	Isaiah 49-50	Rev. 11-12	Psalms 121-125	Proverbs 22
23-Sep	Isaiah 51-52	Rev. 13-14	Psalms 126-130	Proverbs 23
24-Sep	Isaiah 53-54	Rev. 15-16	Psalms 131-135	Proverbs 24
25-Sep	Isaiah 55-56	Rev. 17-18	Psalms 136-140	Proverbs 25
26-Sep	Isaiah 57-58	Rev. 19-20	Psalms 141-145	Proverbs 26
27-Sep	Isaiah 59-60	Rev. 21-22	Psalms 146-150	Proverbs 27
28-Sep	Isaiah 61-62	Matthew 1-2	Psalms 1-5	Proverbs 28
29-Sep	Isaiah 63-64	Matthew 3-4	Psalms 6-10	Proverbs 29
30-Sep	Isaiah 65-66	Matthew 5-6	Psalms 11-15	Proverbs 30
1-Oct	Jeremiah 1-2	Matthew 7-8	Psalms 16-20	Proverbs 1
2-Oct	Jeremiah 3-4	Matthew 9-10	Psalms 21-25	Proverbs 2
3-Oct	Jeremiah 5-6	Matthew 11-12	Psalms 26-30	Proverbs 3
4-Oct	Jeremiah 7-8	Matthew 13-14	Psalms 31-35	Proverbs 4
5-Oct	Jeremiah 9-10	Matthew 15-16	Psalms 36-40	Proverbs 5
6-Oct	Jeremiah 11-12	Matthew 17-18	Psalms 41-45	Proverbs 6
7-Oct	Jeremiah 13-14	Matthew 19-20	Psalms 46-50	Proverbs 7
8-Oct	Jeremiah 15-16	Matthew 21-22	Psalms 51-55	Proverbs 8
9-Oct	Jeremiah 17-18	Matthew 23-24	Psalms 56-60	Proverbs 9
10-Oct	Jeremiah 19-20	Matthew 25-26	Psalms 61-65	Proverbs 10
11-Oct	Jeremiah 21-22	Matthew 27-28	Psalms 66-70	Proverbs 11
12-Oct	Jeremiah 23-24	Mark 1-2	Psalms 71-75	Proverbs 12
13-Oct	Jeremiah 25-26	Mark 3-4	Psalms 76-80	Proverbs 13
14-Oct	Jeremiah 27-28	Mark 5-6	Psalms 81-85	Proverbs 14
15-Oct	Jeremiah 29-30	Mark 7-8	Psalms 86-90	Proverbs 15

"The Five O'clock Club"
Daily Bible Reading Calendar

16-Oct	Jeremiah 31-32	Mark 9-10	Psalms 91-95	Proverbs 16
17-Oct	Jeremiah 33-34	Mark 11-12	Psalms 96-100	Proverbs 17
18-Oct	Jeremiah 35-36	Mark 13-14	Psalms 101-105	Proverbs 18
19-Oct	Jeremiah 37-38	Mark 15-16	Psalms 106-110	Proverbs 19
20-Oct	Jeremiah 39-40	Luke 1-2	Psalms 111-115	Proverbs 20
21-Oct	Jeremiah 41-42	Luke 3-4	Psalms 116-120	Proverbs 21
22-Oct	Jeremiah 43-44	Luke 5-6	Psalms 121-125	Proverbs 22
23-Oct	Jeremiah 45-46	Luke 7-8	Psalms 126-130	Proverbs 23
24-Oct	Jeremiah 47-48	Luke 9-10	Psalms 131-135	Proverbs 24
25-Oct	Jeremiah 49-50	Luke 11-12	Psalms 136-140	Proverbs 25
26-Oct	Jeremiah 51-52	Luke 13-14	Psalms 141-145	Proverbs 26
27-Oct	Lamentations 1-2	Luke 15-16	Psalms 146-150	Proverbs 27
28-Oct	Lamentations 3-5	Luke 17-18	Psalms 1-5	Proverbs 28
29-Oct	Ezekiel 1-2	Luke 19-20	Psalms 6-10	Proverbs 29
30-Oct	Ezekiel 3-4	Luke 21-22	Psalms 11-15	Proverbs 30
31-Oct	Ezekiel 5-6	Luke 23-24	Psalms 16-20	Proverbs 31
1-Nov	Ezekiel 7-8	John 1-2	Psalms 21-25	Proverbs 1
2-Nov	Ezekiel 9-10	John 3-4	Psalms 26-30	Proverbs 2
3-Nov	Ezekiel 11-12	John 5-6	Psalms 31-35	Proverbs 3
4-Nov	Ezekiel 13-14	John 7-8	Psalms 36-40	Proverbs 4
5-Nov	Ezekiel 15-16	John 9-10	Psalms 41-45	Proverbs 5
6-Nov	Ezekiel 17-18	John 11-12	Psalms 46-50	Proverbs 6
7-Nov	Ezekiel 19-20	John 13-14	Psalms 51-55	Proverbs 7
8-Nov	Ezekiel 21-22	John 15-16	Psalms 56-60	Proverbs 8
9-Nov	Ezekiel 23-24	John 17-18	Psalms 61-65	Proverbs 9
10-Nov	Ezekiel 25-26	John 19-20	Psalms 66-70	Proverbs 10
11-Nov	Ezekiel 27-28	John 21	Psalms 71-75	Proverbs 11
12-Nov	Ezekiel 29-30	Acts 1-2	Psalms 76-80	Proverbs 12
13-Nov	Ezekiel 31-32	Acts 3-4	Psalms 81-85	Proverbs 13
14-Nov	Ezekiel 33-34	Acts 5-6	Psalms 86-90	Proverbs 14
15-Nov	Ezekiel 35-36	Acts 7-8	Psalms 91-95	Proverbs 15
16-Nov	Ezekiel 37-38	Acts 9-10	Psalms 96-100	Proverbs 16
17-Nov	Ezekiel 39-40	Acts 11-12	Psalms 101-105	Proverbs 17
18-Nov	Ezekiel 41-42	Acts 13-14	Psalms 106-110	Proverbs 18
19-Nov	Ezekiel 43-44	Acts 15-16	Psalms 111-115	Proverbs 19
20-Nov	Ezekiel 45-46	Acts 17-18	Psalms 116-120	Proverbs 20
21-Nov	Ezekiel 47-48	Acts 19-20	Psalms 121-125	Proverbs 21

"The Five O'clock Club"
Daily Bible Reading Calendar

22-Nov	Daniel 1-2	Acts 21-22	Psalms 126-130	Proverbs 22
23-Nov	Daniel 3-4	Acts 23-24	Psalms 131-135	Proverbs 23
24-Nov	Daniel 5-6	Acts 25-26	Psalms 136-140	Proverbs 24
25-Nov	Daniel 7-8	Acts 27-28	Psalms 141-145	Proverbs 25
26-Nov	Daniel 9-10	Romans 1-2	Psalms 146-150	Proverbs 26
27-Nov	Daniel 11-12	Romans 3-4	Psalms 1-5	Proverbs 27
28-Nov	Hosea 1-2	Romans 5-6	Psalms 6-10	Proverbs 28
29-Nov	Hosea 3-4	Romans 7-8	Psalms 11-15	Proverbs 29
30-Nov	Hosea 5-6	Romans 9-10	Psalms 16-20	Proverbs 30
1-Dec	Hosea 7-8	Romans 11-12	Psalms 21-25	Proverbs 1
2-Dec	Hosea 9-10	Romans 13-14	Psalms 26-30	Proverbs 2
3-Dec	Hosea 11-12	Romans 15-16	Psalms 31-35	Proverbs 3
4-Dec	Hosea 13-14	1 Cor. 1-2	Psalms 36-40	Proverbs 4
5-Dec	Joel 1-3	1 Cor. 3-4	Psalms 41-45	Proverbs 5
6-Dec	Amos 1-2	1 Cor. 5-6	Psalms 46-50	Proverbs 6
7-Dec	Amos 3-4	1 Cor. 7-8	Psalms 51-55	Proverbs 7
8-Dec	Amos 5-6	1 Cor. 9-10	Psalms 56-60	Proverbs 8
9-Dec	Amos 7-9	1 Cor. 11-12	Psalms 61-65	Proverbs 9
10-Dec	Obadiah 1	1 Cor. 13-14	Psalms 66-70	Proverbs 10
11-Dec	Jonah 1-2	1 Cor. 15-16	Psalms 71-75	Proverbs 11
12-Dec	Jonah 3-4	2 Cor 1-2	Psalms 76-80	Proverbs 12
13-Dec	Micah 1-2	2 Cor. 3-4	Psalms 81-85	Proverbs 13
14-Dec	Micah 3-4	2 Cor. 5-6	Psalms 86-90	Proverbs 14
15-Dec	Micah 5-7	2 Cor. 7-8	Psalms 91-95	Proverbs 15
16-Dec	Nahum 1-3	2 Cor. 9-10	Psalms 96-100	Proverbs 16
17-Dec	Habakkuk 1-3	2 Cor. 11-12	Psalms 101-105	Proverbs 17
18-Dec	Zephaniah 1-3	2 Cor. 13	Psalms 106-110	Proverbs 18
19-Dec	Haggai 1-2	Galatians 1-2	Psalms 111-115	Proverbs 19
20-Dec	Zechariah 1-2	Galatians 3-4	Psalms 116-120	Proverbs 20
21-Dec	Zechariah 3-4	Galatians 5-6	Psalms 121-125	Proverbs 21
22-Dec	Zechariah 5-6	Ephesians 1-2	Psalms 126-130	Proverbs 22
23-Dec	Zechariah 7-8	Ephesians 3-4	Psalms 131-135	Proverbs 23
24-Dec	Zechariah 9-10	Ephesians 5-6	Psalms 136-140	Proverbs 24
25-Dec	**Merry Christmas!**	Philippians 1-2	Psalms 141-145	Proverbs 25

Isaiah 9:6 - 7 (KJV) For unto us a child is born, unto us a son is given: and the government shall be upon his shoulder: and his name shall be called Wonderful, Counsellor, The mighty God, The everlasting Father, The Prince of Peace. Of the increase of his government and peace there shall be no end . . .

"The Five O'clock Club"
Daily Bible Reading Calendar

26-Dec	Zechariah 11-12	Philippians 3-4	Psalms 146-150	Proverbs 26
27-Dec	Zechariah 13-14	Colossians 1-2	Psalms 1-5	Proverbs 27
28-Dec	Malachi 1	Colossians 3-4	Psalms 6-10	Proverbs 28
29-Dec	Malachi 2	1 Thess. 1-2	Psalms 11-15	Proverbs 29
30-Dec	Malachi 3	1 Thess. 3-4	Psalms 16-20	Proverbs 30
31-Dec	Malachi 4	1 Thess. 5	Psalms 21-25	Proverbs 31

Congratulations! You have just finished the calendar year. A new year is upon you and God has an amazing plan to unfold for your upcoming new year! This is a good seasonal time to reflect on all of your goals and visions that you have written down, and to ask God for special understanding for the coming year. January is a perfect time to fast, pray and seek God concerning your new short term one year goals, as well as your medium and long term goals.

PHYSICAL

Your Kingdom Domain

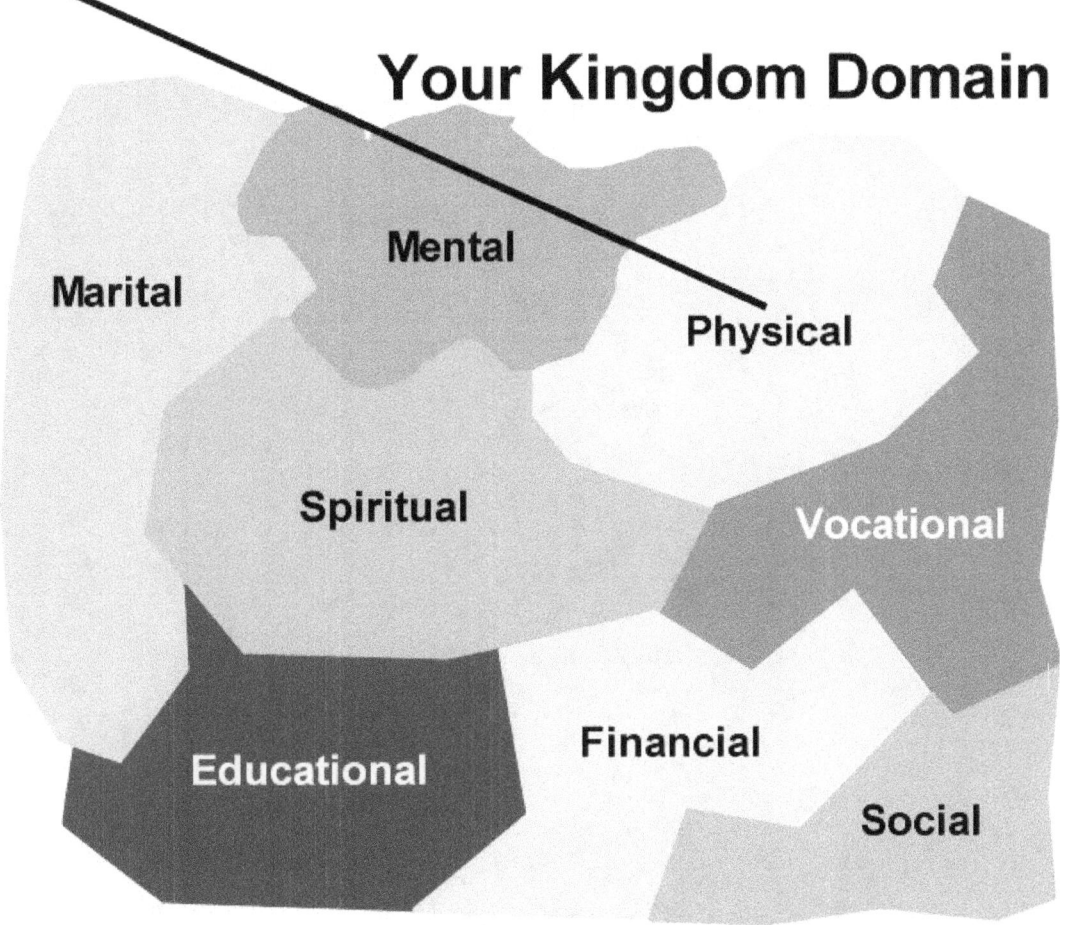

Prov. 15:22 (NIV) Plans fail for lack of counsel, but with many advisers they succeed.

Keywords That May Help You With Your Goals: Health, Fitness, Nutrition, Weight, Exercise, Cleanliness, Hygiene, Rest, Appearance, Grooming, Clothing, Teeth, Vacation, Sports, Medical, Prescriptions, Food, Self Control, Environment, Home, Body, House, Real Estate, Transportation, Equipment, Supplies.

PHYSICAL GOALS: Short, Medium, Long Term

Create your target goals now. Modify them throughout the year as you walk through God's Word & daily meditation.

Goals *Physical*

Short Term Goals – One Year Or Less   Date Created:_____

1._____

2._____

3._____

Medium Term Goals – Five Years   Date Created:_____

1._____

2._____

3._____

Long Term Goals – Ten Years   Date Created:_____

1._____

2._____

3._____

Long Term Goals – Twenty Years   Date Created:_____

1._____

2._____

3._____

Long Term Goals – Fifty Years   Date Created:_____

1._____

2._____

3._____

Psalms 119:105 "Thy word is a lamp unto my feet, and a light unto my path."

© 2012 Mighty Eagle Publishing   All Rights Reserved
www.mightyeagle.com   www.doctordanieldaves.com

MIGHTY EAGLE PUBLISHING

PHYSICAL GOALS: Continued . . .

Goals *Physical*

Notes:_____

_____

_____

_____

_____

_____

_____

_____

_____

_____

_____

_____

_____

_____

_____

_____

_____

_____

_____

_____

_____

_____

_____

_____

_____

_____

Psalms 119:105 "Thy word is a lamp unto my feet, and a light unto my path."

DAILY NOTES AND JOURNAL ENTRIES: *(Remember to date your journal entries)*

Habakkuk 2:2 "Write the vision, and make it plain upon tables, that he may run that readeth it."

DAILY NOTES AND JOURNAL ENTRIES: *(Remember to date your journal entries)*

Psalms 119:105 "Thy word is a lamp unto my feet, and a light unto my path."

DAILY NOTES AND JOURNAL ENTRIES: *(Remember to date your journal entries)*

Physical

Habakkuk 2:2 "Write the vision, and make it plain upon tables, that he may run that readeth it."

© 2012 Mighty Eagle Publishing   All Rights Reserved
www.mightyeagle.com   www.doctordanieldaves.com

DAILY NOTES AND JOURNAL ENTRIES: *(Remember to date your journal entries)*

Psalms 119:105 "Thy word is a lamp unto my feet, and a light unto my path."

DAILY NOTES AND JOURNAL ENTRIES: *(Remember to date your journal entries)*

Physical

_____
_____
_____
_____
_____
_____
_____
_____
_____
_____
_____
_____
_____
_____
_____
_____
_____
_____
_____
_____
_____
_____
_____
_____
_____
_____
_____

Habakkuk 2:2 "Write the vision, and make it plain upon tables, that he may run that readeth it."

© 2012 Mighty Eagle Publishing   All Rights Reserved
www.mightyeagle.com   www.doctordanieldaves.com

DAILY NOTES AND JOURNAL ENTRIES: *(Remember to date your journal entries)*

Psalms 119:105 "Thy word is a lamp unto my feet, and a light unto my path."

© 2012 Mighty Eagle Publishing   All Rights Reserved
www.mightyeagle.com   www.doctordanieldaves.com

DAILY NOTES AND JOURNAL ENTRIES: *(Remember to date your journal entries)*

Physical

Habakkuk 2:2 "Write the vision, and make it plain upon tables, that he may run that readeth it."

DAILY NOTES AND JOURNAL ENTRIES: *(Remember to date your journal entries)*

Psalms 119:105 "Thy word is a lamp unto my feet, and a light unto my path."

DAILY NOTES AND JOURNAL ENTRIES: *(Remember to date your journal entries)*

Habakkuk 2:2 *"Write the vision, and make it plain upon tables, that he may run that readeth it."*

© 2012 Mighty Eagle Publishing   All Rights Reserved
www.mightyeagle.com   www.doctordanieldaves.com

DAILY NOTES AND JOURNAL ENTRIES: *(Remember to date your journal entries)*

Psalms 119:105 "Thy word is a lamp unto my feet, and a light unto my path."

DAILY NOTES AND JOURNAL ENTRIES: *(Remember to date your journal entries)*

Physical

Habakkuk 2:2 "Write the vision, and make it plain upon tables, that he may run that readeth it."

DAILY NOTES AND JOURNAL ENTRIES: *(Remember to date your journal entries)*

Psalms 119:105 "Thy word is a lamp unto my feet, and a light unto my path."

DAILY NOTES AND JOURNAL ENTRIES: *(Remember to date your journal entries)*

Physical

Habakkuk 2:2 "Write the vision, and make it plain upon tables, that he may run that readeth it."

© 2012 Mighty Eagle Publishing   All Rights Reserved
www.mightyeagle.com   www.doctordanieldaves.com

DAILY NOTES AND JOURNAL ENTRIES: *(Remember to date your journal entries)*

Psalms 119:105 "Thy word is a lamp unto my feet, and a light unto my path."

© 2012 Mighty Eagle Publishing   All Rights Reserved
www.mightyeagle.com   www.doctordanieldaves.com

DAILY NOTES AND JOURNAL ENTRIES: *(Remember to date your journal entries)*

Physical

Habakkuk 2:2 "Write the vision, and make it plain upon tables, that he may run that readeth it."

DAILY NOTES AND JOURNAL ENTRIES: *(Remember to date your journal entries)*

Psalms 119:105 "Thy word is a lamp unto my feet, and a light unto my path."

DAILY NOTES AND JOURNAL ENTRIES: *(Remember to date your journal entries)*

Physical

Habakkuk 2:2 "Write the vision, and make it plain upon tables, that he may run that readeth it."

© 2012 Mighty Eagle Publishing   All Rights Reserved
www.mightyeagle.com   www.doctordanieldaves.com

DAILY NOTES AND JOURNAL ENTRIES: *(Remember to date your journal entries)*

Psalms 119:105 "Thy word is a lamp unto my feet, and a light unto my path."

DAILY NOTES AND JOURNAL ENTRIES: *(Remember to date your journal entries)*

Physical

Habakkuk 2:2 "Write the vision, and make it plain upon tables, that he may run that readeth it."

DAILY NOTES AND JOURNAL ENTRIES: *(Remember to date your journal entries)*

Psalms 119:105 "Thy word is a lamp unto my feet, and a light unto my path."

DAILY NOTES AND JOURNAL ENTRIES: *(Remember to date your journal entries)*

Habakkuk 2:2 "Write the vision, and make it plain upon tables, that he may run that readeth it."

DAILY NOTES AND JOURNAL ENTRIES: *(Remember to date your journal entries)*

Psalms 119:105 "Thy word is a lamp unto my feet, and a light unto my path."

© 2012 Mighty Eagle Publishing   All Rights Reserved
www.mightyeagle.com   www.doctordanieldaves.com

DAILY NOTES AND JOURNAL ENTRIES: *(Remember to date your journal entries)*

Physical

Habakkuk 2:2 "Write the vision, and make it plain upon tables, that he may run that readeth it."

DAILY NOTES AND JOURNAL ENTRIES: *(Remember to date your journal entries)*

Psalms 119:105 "Thy word is a lamp unto my feet, and a light unto my path."

MENTAL – MENTAL – MENTAL – MENTAL – MENTAL – MENTAL

Mental

MENTAL

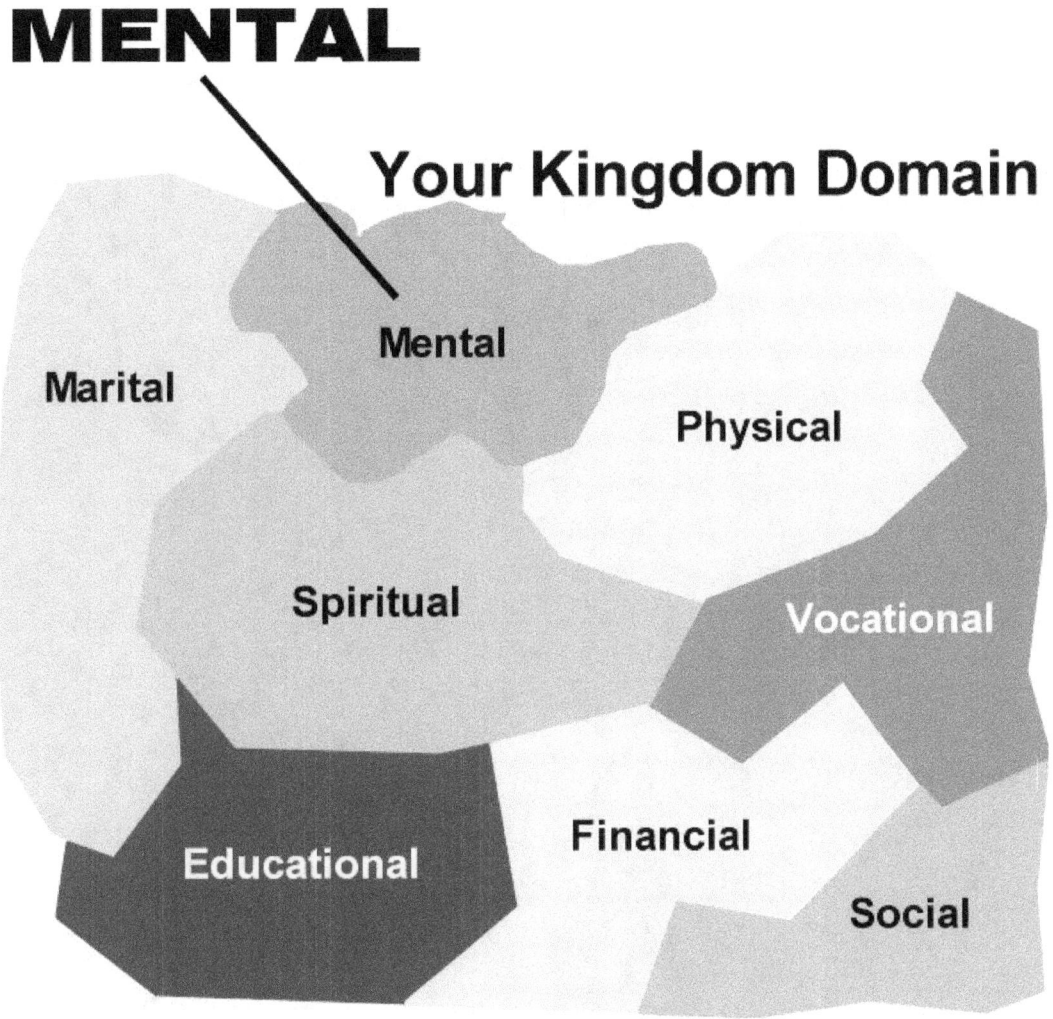

Your Kingdom Domain

Psalms 20:4 (NIV) May he give you the desire of your heart and make all your plans succeed.

Keywords That may Help You With Your Goals: Mind, Will, Emotions, Meditation, Rest, peace, Calm, Double Minded, Single Minded, Focus, Positive, Morals, Imagination, Intellect, Reasoning, Thinking, Thought, A.D.D., A.D.H.D., Happiness, Joy

MENTAL GOALS: Short, Medium, Long Term

Create your target goals now. Modify them throughout the year as you walk through God's Word & daily meditation.

Short Term Goals – One Year Or Less   Date Created:_____

1._____
2._____
3._____

Medium Term Goals – Five Years   Date Created:_____

1._____
2._____
3._____

Long Term Goals – Ten Years   Date Created:_____

1._____
2._____
3._____

Long Term Goals – Twenty Years   Date Created:_____

1._____
2._____
3._____

Long Term Goals – Fifty Years   Date Created:_____

1._____
2._____
3._____

Psalms 119:105 "Thy word is a lamp unto my feet, and a light unto my path."

© 2012 Mighty Eagle Publishing   All Rights Reserved
www.mightyeagle.com   www.doctordanieldaves.com

MENTAL GOALS: Continued . . .

Notes:_____

Psalms 119:105 "Thy word is a lamp unto my feet, and a light unto my path."

DAILY NOTES AND JOURNAL ENTRIES: *(Remember to date your journal entries)*

Mental

Habakkuk 2:2 "Write the vision, and make it plain upon tables, that he may run that readeth it."

DAILY NOTES AND JOURNAL ENTRIES: *(Remember to date your journal entries)*

Psalms 119:105 "Thy word is a lamp unto my feet, and a light unto my path."

DAILY NOTES AND JOURNAL ENTRIES: *(Remember to date your journal entries)*

Mental

Habakkuk 2:2 "Write the vision, and make it plain upon tables, that he may run that readeth it."

© 2012 Mighty Eagle Publishing   All Rights Reserved
www.mightyeagle.com   www.doctordanieldaves.com

DAILY NOTES AND JOURNAL ENTRIES: *(Remember to date your journal entries)*

Psalms 119:105 "Thy word is a lamp unto my feet, and a light unto my path."

© 2012 Mighty Eagle Publishing   All Rights Reserved
www.mightyeagle.com   www.doctordanieldaves.com

DAILY NOTES AND JOURNAL ENTRIES: *(Remember to date your journal entries)*

Mental

Habakkuk 2:2 "Write the vision, and make it plain upon tables, that he may run that readeth it."

© 2012 Mighty Eagle Publishing   All Rights Reserved
www.mightyeagle.com   www.doctordanieldaves.com

DAILY NOTES AND JOURNAL ENTRIES: *(Remember to date your journal entries)*

Psalms 119:105 "Thy word is a lamp unto my feet, and a light unto my path."

DAILY NOTES AND JOURNAL ENTRIES: *(Remember to date your journal entries)*

Mental

Habakkuk 2:2 "Write the vision, and make it plain upon tables, that he may run that readeth it."

DAILY NOTES AND JOURNAL ENTRIES: *(Remember to date your journal entries)*

Psalms 119:105 "Thy word is a lamp unto my feet, and a light unto my path."

© 2012 Mighty Eagle Publishing   All Rights Reserved
www.mightyeagle.com   www.doctordanieldaves.com

DAILY NOTES AND JOURNAL ENTRIES: *(Remember to date your journal entries)*

Mental

Habakkuk 2:2 "Write the vision, and make it plain upon tables, that he may run that readeth it."

© 2012 Mighty Eagle Publishing   All Rights Reserved
www.mightyeagle.com   www.doctordanieldaves.com

DAILY NOTES AND JOURNAL ENTRIES: *(Remember to date your journal entries)*

Psalms 119:105 "Thy word is a lamp unto my feet, and a light unto my path."

© 2012 Mighty Eagle Publishing   All Rights Reserved
www.mightyeagle.com   www.doctordanieldaves.com

DAILY NOTES AND JOURNAL ENTRIES: *(Remember to date your journal entries)*

Mental

Habakkuk 2:2 "Write the vision, and make it plain upon tables, that he may run that readeth it."

DAILY NOTES AND JOURNAL ENTRIES: *(Remember to date your journal entries)*

Psalms 119:105 "Thy word is a lamp unto my feet, and a light unto my path."

DAILY NOTES AND JOURNAL ENTRIES: *(Remember to date your journal entries)*

Mental

Habakkuk 2:2 "Write the vision, and make it plain upon tables, that he may run that readeth it."

DAILY NOTES AND JOURNAL ENTRIES: *(Remember to date your journal entries)*

Psalms 119:105 "Thy word is a lamp unto my feet, and a light unto my path."

DAILY NOTES AND JOURNAL ENTRIES: *(Remember to date your journal entries)*

Mental

Habakkuk 2:2 "Write the vision, and make it plain upon tables, that he may run that readeth it."

DAILY NOTES AND JOURNAL ENTRIES: *(Remember to date your journal entries)*

Psalms 119:105 "Thy word is a lamp unto my feet, and a light unto my path."

DAILY NOTES AND JOURNAL ENTRIES: *(Remember to date your journal entries)*

Mental

Habakkuk 2:2 "Write the vision, and make it plain upon tables, that he may run that readeth it."

DAILY NOTES AND JOURNAL ENTRIES: *(Remember to date your journal entries)*

Psalms 119:105 "Thy word is a lamp unto my feet, and a light unto my path."

DAILY NOTES AND JOURNAL ENTRIES: *(Remember to date your journal entries)*

Mental

Habakkuk 2:2 "Write the vision, and make it plain upon tables, that he may run that readeth it."

© 2012 Mighty Eagle Publishing   All Rights Reserved
www.mightyeagle.com   www.doctordanieldaves.com

DAILY NOTES AND JOURNAL ENTRIES: *(Remember to date your journal entries)*

Psalms 119:105 "Thy word is a lamp unto my feet, and a light unto my path."

DAILY NOTES AND JOURNAL ENTRIES: *(Remember to date your journal entries)*

Mental

Habakkuk 2:2 "Write the vision, and make it plain upon tables, that he may run that readeth it."

© 2012 Mighty Eagle Publishing   All Rights Reserved
www.mightyeagle.com   www.doctordanieldaves.com

DAILY NOTES AND JOURNAL ENTRIES: *(Remember to date your journal entries)*

Psalms 119:105 "Thy word is a lamp unto my feet, and a light unto my path."

DAILY NOTES AND JOURNAL ENTRIES: *(Remember to date your journal entries)*

Mental

Habakkuk 2:2 "Write the vision, and make it plain upon tables, that he may run that readeth it."

© 2012 Mighty Eagle Publishing   All Rights Reserved
www.mightyeagle.com   www.doctordanieldaves.com

DAILY NOTES AND JOURNAL ENTRIES: *(Remember to date your journal entries)*

Psalms 119:105 "Thy word is a lamp unto my feet, and a light unto my path."

SPIRITUAL – SPIRITUAL – SPIRITUAL – SPIRITUAL – SPIRITUAL

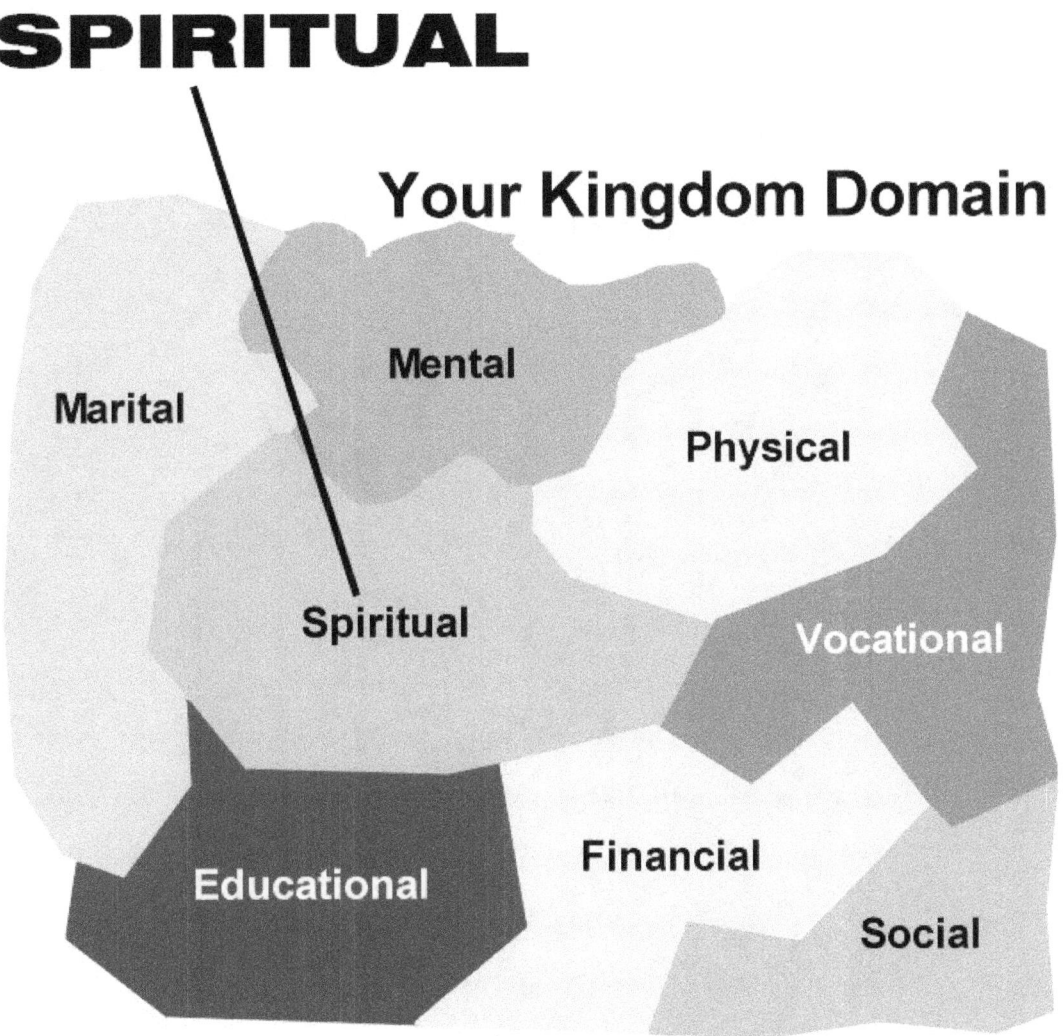

Psalms 20:4 (NIV) May he give you the desire of your heart and make all your plans succeed.

Keywords That may Help You With Your Goals: Prayer, Fellowship With God, Fasting, Bible, Meditation, Salvation, Holy Spirit, Communion, Pure, Cleanse, Holy, Worship, Devotion, Blessing, Miracles, Church, Supernatural, Heaven, Hell, Missions

SPIRITUAL GOALS: Short, Medium, Long Term

Create your target goals now. Modify them throughout the year as you walk through God's Word & daily meditation.

Short Term Goals – One Year Or Less   Date Created:_____

1._____

2._____

3._____

Medium Term Goals – Five Years   Date Created:_____

1._____

2._____

3._____

Long Term Goals – Ten Years   Date Created:_____

1._____

2._____

3._____

Long Term Goals – Twenty Years   Date Created:_____

1._____

2._____

3._____

Long Term Goals – Fifty Years   Date Created:_____

1._____

2._____

3._____

*Psalms 119:105 "Thy word is a lamp unto my feet, and a light unto my path."*_____

© 2012 Mighty Eagle Publishing   All Rights Reserved
www.mightyeagle.com   www.doctordanieldaves.com

SPIRITUAL GOALS: Continued . . .

Notes:_____

Goals *Spiritual*

Psalms 119:105 "Thy word is a lamp unto my feet, and a light unto my path."

© 2012 Mighty Eagle Publishing   All Rights Reserved
www.mightyeagle.com   www.doctordanieldaves.com

DAILY NOTES AND JOURNAL ENTRIES: *(Remember to date your journal entries)*

Spiritual

Habakkuk 2:2 "Write the vision, and make it plain upon tables, that he may run that readeth it."

© 2012 Mighty Eagle Publishing   All Rights Reserved
www.mightyeagle.com   www.doctordanieldaves.com

DAILY NOTES AND JOURNAL ENTRIES: *(Remember to date your journal entries)*

Psalms 119:105 "Thy word is a lamp unto my feet, and a light unto my path."

DAILY NOTES AND JOURNAL ENTRIES: *(Remember to date your journal entries)*

Spiritual

Habakkuk 2:2 "Write the vision, and make it plain upon tables, that he may run that readeth it."

© 2012 Mighty Eagle Publishing   All Rights Reserved
www.mightyeagle.com   www.doctordanieldaves.com

DAILY NOTES AND JOURNAL ENTRIES: *(Remember to date your journal entries)*

Psalms 119:105 "Thy word is a lamp unto my feet, and a light unto my path."

© 2012 Mighty Eagle Publishing   All Rights Reserved
www.mightyeagle.com   www.doctordanieldaves.com

DAILY NOTES AND JOURNAL ENTRIES: *(Remember to date your journal entries)*

Spiritual

Habakkuk 2:2 "Write the vision, and make it plain upon tables, that he may run that readeth it."

© 2012 Mighty Eagle Publishing   All Rights Reserved
www.mightyeagle.com   www.doctordanieldaves.com

DAILY NOTES AND JOURNAL ENTRIES: *(Remember to date your journal entries)*

Psalms 119:105 "Thy word is a lamp unto my feet, and a light unto my path."

DAILY NOTES AND JOURNAL ENTRIES: *(Remember to date your journal entries)*

Spiritual

Habakkuk 2:2 "Write the vision, and make it plain upon tables, that he may run that readeth it."

© 2012 Mighty Eagle Publishing   All Rights Reserved
www.mightyeagle.com   www.doctordanieldaves.com

DAILY NOTES AND JOURNAL ENTRIES: *(Remember to date your journal entries)*

Psalms 119:105 "Thy word is a lamp unto my feet, and a light unto my path."

© 2012 Mighty Eagle Publishing   All Rights Reserved
www.mightyeagle.com   www.doctordanieldaves.com

DAILY NOTES AND JOURNAL ENTRIES: *(Remember to date your journal entries)*

Spiritual

Habakkuk 2:2 "Write the vision, and make it plain upon tables, that he may run that readeth it."

DAILY NOTES AND JOURNAL ENTRIES: *(Remember to date your journal entries)*

Psalms 119:105 "Thy word is a lamp unto my feet, and a light unto my path."

DAILY NOTES AND JOURNAL ENTRIES: *(Remember to date your journal entries)*

Spiritual

Habakkuk 2:2 "Write the vision, and make it plain upon tables, that he may run that readeth it."

© 2012 Mighty Eagle Publishing   All Rights Reserved
www.mightyeagle.com   www.doctordanieldaves.com

DAILY NOTES AND JOURNAL ENTRIES: *(Remember to date your journal entries)*

Psalms 119:105 "Thy word is a lamp unto my feet, and a light unto my path."

DAILY NOTES AND JOURNAL ENTRIES: *(Remember to date your journal entries)*

Spiritual

Habakkuk 2:2 "Write the vision, and make it plain upon tables, that he may run that readeth it."

© 2012 Mighty Eagle Publishing   All Rights Reserved
www.mightyeagle.com   www.doctordanieldaves.com

DAILY NOTES AND JOURNAL ENTRIES: *(Remember to date your journal entries)*

Psalms 119:105 "Thy word is a lamp unto my feet, and a light unto my path."

© 2012 Mighty Eagle Publishing   All Rights Reserved
www.mightyeagle.com   www.doctordanieldaves.com

DAILY NOTES AND JOURNAL ENTRIES: *(Remember to date your journal entries)*

Spiritual

Habakkuk 2:2 "Write the vision, and make it plain upon tables, that he may run that readeth it."

© 2012 Mighty Eagle Publishing   All Rights Reserved
www.mightyeagle.com   www.doctordanieldaves.com

DAILY NOTES AND JOURNAL ENTRIES: *(Remember to date your journal entries)*

Psalms 119:105 "Thy word is a lamp unto my feet, and a light unto my path."

DAILY NOTES AND JOURNAL ENTRIES: *(Remember to date your journal entries)*

Spiritual

Habakkuk 2:2 "Write the vision, and make it plain upon tables, that he may run that readeth it."

DAILY NOTES AND JOURNAL ENTRIES: *(Remember to date your journal entries)*

Psalms 119:105 "Thy word is a lamp unto my feet, and a light unto my path."

© 2012 Mighty Eagle Publishing   All Rights Reserved
www.mightyeagle.com   www.doctordanieldaves.com

DAILY NOTES AND JOURNAL ENTRIES: *(Remember to date your journal entries)*

Spiritual

Habakkuk 2:2 "Write the vision, and make it plain upon tables, that he may run that readeth it."

© 2012 Mighty Eagle Publishing   All Rights Reserved
www.mightyeagle.com   www.doctordanieldaves.com

DAILY NOTES AND JOURNAL ENTRIES: *(Remember to date your journal entries)*

Psalms 119:105 "Thy word is a lamp unto my feet, and a light unto my path."

© 2012 Mighty Eagle Publishing   All Rights Reserved
www.mightyeagle.com   www.doctordanieldaves.com

DAILY NOTES AND JOURNAL ENTRIES: *(Remember to date your journal entries)*

Spiritual

Habakkuk 2:2 "Write the vision, and make it plain upon tables, that he may run that readeth it."

DAILY NOTES AND JOURNAL ENTRIES: *(Remember to date your journal entries)*

Psalms 119:105 "Thy word is a lamp unto my feet, and a light unto my path."

© 2012 Mighty Eagle Publishing   All Rights Reserved
www.mightyeagle.com   www.doctordanieldaves.com

DAILY NOTES AND JOURNAL ENTRIES: *(Remember to date your journal entries)*

Spiritual

Habakkuk 2:2 "Write the vision, and make it plain upon tables, that he may run that readeth it."

© 2012 Mighty Eagle Publishing   All Rights Reserved
www.mightyeagle.com   www.doctordanieldaves.com

DAILY NOTES AND JOURNAL ENTRIES: *(Remember to date your journal entries)*

Psalms 119:105 "Thy word is a lamp unto my feet, and a light unto my path."

© 2012 Mighty Eagle Publishing   All Rights Reserved
www.mightyeagle.com   www.doctordanieldaves.com

SOCIAL – SOCIAL – SOCIAL – SOCIAL – SOCIAL – SOCIAL –

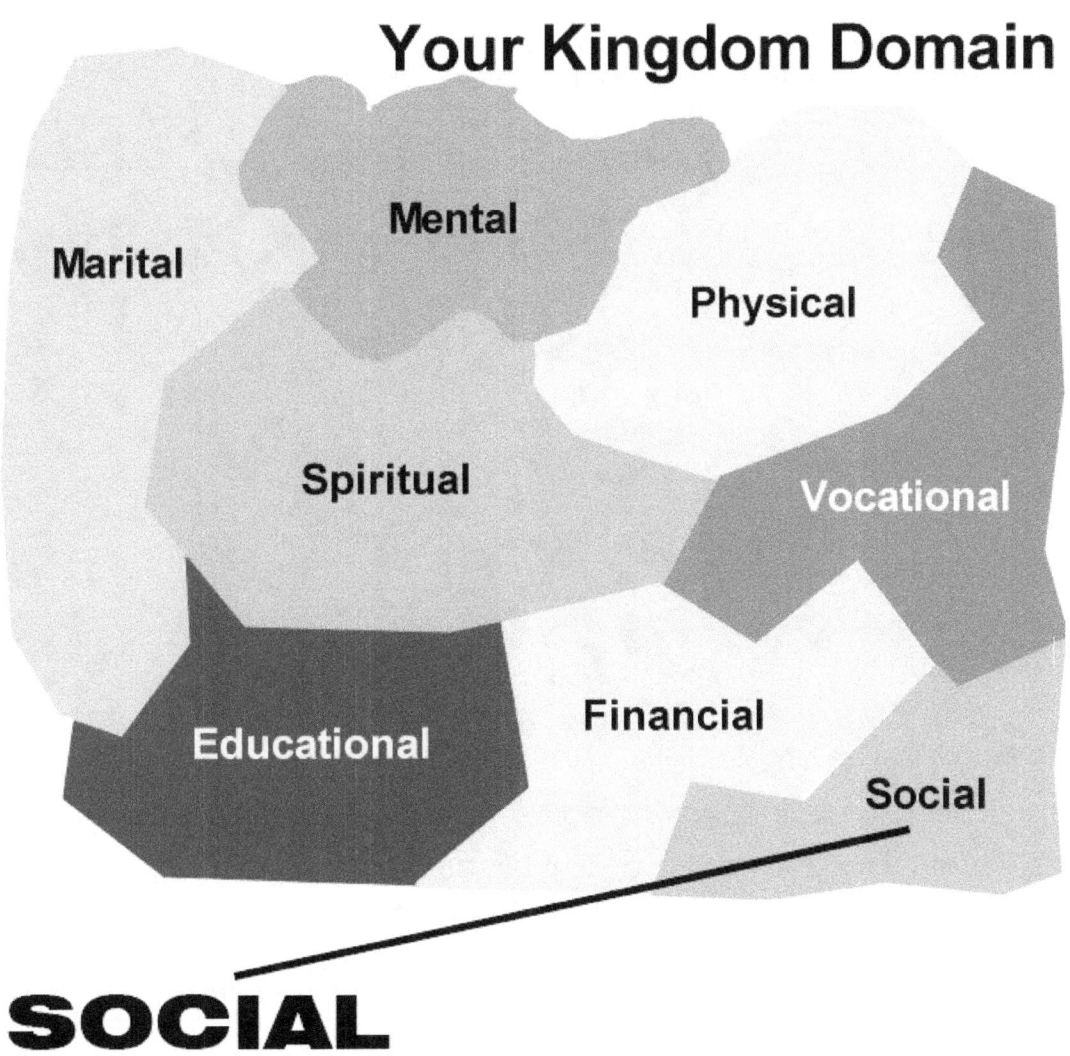

Prov. 16:3 (NIV) Commit to the LORD whatever you do, and your plans will succeed.

Keywords That may Help You With Your Goals: Talk, Friends, Communication, Social Skills, Enemies, Forgiveness, Apology, Repentance, Laughter, Joy, Peace, Associations, Manners, Etiquette, Civil, Communion, Entertainment, Group, Hospitable, Mannerly, Neighborly, Pleasant, Polite, Popular, Sociable, Society.

SOCIAL GOALS: Short, Medium, Long Term

Create your target goals now. Modify them throughout the year as you walk through God's Word & daily meditation.

Short Term Goals – One Year Or Less   *Date Created:*_____

1._____

2._____

3._____

Medium Term Goals – Five Years   *Date Created:*_____

1._____

2._____

3._____

Long Term Goals – Ten Years   *Date Created:*_____

1._____

2._____

3._____

Long Term Goals – Twenty Years   *Date Created:*_____

1._____

2._____

3._____

Long Term Goals – Fifty Years   *Date Created:*_____

1._____

2._____

3._____

Psalms 119:105 "Thy word is a lamp unto my feet, and a light unto my path."

© 2012 Mighty Eagle Publishing   All Rights Reserved
www.mightyeagle.com   www.doctordanieldaves.com

SOCIAL GOALS: Continued . . .

Notes:_____

Goals *Social*

Psalms 119:105 "Thy word is a lamp unto my feet, and a light unto my path."

© 2012 Mighty Eagle Publishing   All Rights Reserved
www.mightyeagle.com   www.doctordanieldaves.com

DAILY NOTES AND JOURNAL ENTRIES: *(Remember to date your journal entries)*

Social

Habakkuk 2:2 "*Write the vision, and make it plain upon tables, that he may run that readeth it.*"

© 2012 Mighty Eagle Publishing   All Rights Reserved
www.mightyeagle.com   www.doctordanieldaves.com

DAILY NOTES AND JOURNAL ENTRIES: *(Remember to date your journal entries)*

Psalms 119:105 "*Thy word is a lamp unto my feet, and a light unto my path.*"

© 2012 Mighty Eagle Publishing   All Rights Reserved
www.mightyeagle.com   www.doctordanieldaves.com

DAILY NOTES AND JOURNAL ENTRIES: *(Remember to date your journal entries)*

Social

Habakkuk 2:2 "Write the vision, and make it plain upon tables, that he may run that readeth it."

DAILY NOTES AND JOURNAL ENTRIES: *(Remember to date your journal entries)*

Psalms 119:105 "Thy word is a lamp unto my feet, and a light unto my path."

DAILY NOTES AND JOURNAL ENTRIES: *(Remember to date your journal entries)*

Social

Habakkuk 2:2 "Write the vision, and make it plain upon tables, that he may run that readeth it."

© 2012 Mighty Eagle Publishing   All Rights Reserved
www.mightyeagle.com   www.doctordanieldaves.com

DAILY NOTES AND JOURNAL ENTRIES: *(Remember to date your journal entries)*

Psalms 119:105 "Thy word is a lamp unto my feet, and a light unto my path."

DAILY NOTES AND JOURNAL ENTRIES: *(Remember to date your journal entries)*

Social

Habakkuk 2:2 "Write the vision, and make it plain upon tables, that he may run that readeth it."

© 2012 Mighty Eagle Publishing   All Rights Reserved
www.mightyeagle.com   www.doctordanieldaves.com

DAILY NOTES AND JOURNAL ENTRIES: *(Remember to date your journal entries)*

Psalms 119:105 "Thy word is a lamp unto my feet, and a light unto my path."

DAILY NOTES AND JOURNAL ENTRIES: *(Remember to date your journal entries)*

Habakkuk 2:2 "Write the vision, and make it plain upon tables, that he may run that readeth it."

© 2012 Mighty Eagle Publishing   All Rights Reserved
www.mightyeagle.com   www.doctordanieldaves.com

DAILY NOTES AND JOURNAL ENTRIES: *(Remember to date your journal entries)*

Psalms 119:105 "Thy word is a lamp unto my feet, and a light unto my path."

DAILY NOTES AND JOURNAL ENTRIES: *(Remember to date your journal entries)*

Social

Habakkuk 2:2 "Write the vision, and make it plain upon tables, that he may run that readeth it."

© 2012 Mighty Eagle Publishing   All Rights Reserved
www.mightyeagle.com   www.doctordanieldaves.com

DAILY NOTES AND JOURNAL ENTRIES: *(Remember to date your journal entries)*

Psalms 119:105 "Thy word is a lamp unto my feet, and a light unto my path."

DAILY NOTES AND JOURNAL ENTRIES: *(Remember to date your journal entries)*

Habakkuk 2:2 "Write the vision, and make it plain upon tables, that he may run that readeth it."

DAILY NOTES AND JOURNAL ENTRIES: *(Remember to date your journal entries)*

Psalms 119:105 "Thy word is a lamp unto my feet, and a light unto my path."

© 2012 Mighty Eagle Publishing   All Rights Reserved
www.mightyeagle.com   www.doctordanieldaves.com

DAILY NOTES AND JOURNAL ENTRIES: *(Remember to date your journal entries)*

Habakkuk 2:2 "Write the vision, and make it plain upon tables, that he may run that readeth it."

DAILY NOTES AND JOURNAL ENTRIES: *(Remember to date your journal entries)*

Psalms 119:105 "Thy word is a lamp unto my feet, and a light unto my path."

DAILY NOTES AND JOURNAL ENTRIES: *(Remember to date your journal entries)*

Social

Habakkuk 2:2 "*Write the vision, and make it plain upon tables, that he may run that readeth it.*"

© 2012 Mighty Eagle Publishing   All Rights Reserved
www.mightyeagle.com   www.doctordanieldaves.com

DAILY NOTES AND JOURNAL ENTRIES: *(Remember to date your journal entries)*

Psalms 119:105 "Thy word is a lamp unto my feet, and a light unto my path."

DAILY NOTES AND JOURNAL ENTRIES: *(Remember to date your journal entries)*

Social

Habakkuk 2:2 "Write the vision, and make it plain upon tables, that he may run that readeth it."

© 2012 Mighty Eagle Publishing   All Rights Reserved
www.mightyeagle.com   www.doctordanieldaves.com

DAILY NOTES AND JOURNAL ENTRIES: *(Remember to date your journal entries)*

Psalms 119:105 "Thy word is a lamp unto my feet, and a light unto my path."

DAILY NOTES AND JOURNAL ENTRIES: *(Remember to date your journal entries)*

Social

Habakkuk 2:2 "Write the vision, and make it plain upon tables, that he may run that readeth it."

© 2012 Mighty Eagle Publishing   All Rights Reserved
www.mightyeagle.com   www.doctordanieldaves.com

DAILY NOTES AND JOURNAL ENTRIES: *(Remember to date your journal entries)*

Psalms 119:105 "Thy word is a lamp unto my feet, and a light unto my path."

DAILY NOTES AND JOURNAL ENTRIES: *(Remember to date your journal entries)*

Social

Habakkuk 2:2 "Write the vision, and make it plain upon tables, that he may run that readeth it."

© 2012 Mighty Eagle Publishing   All Rights Reserved
www.mightyeagle.com   www.doctordanieldaves.com

DAILY NOTES AND JOURNAL ENTRIES: *(Remember to date your journal entries)*

Psalms 119:105 "Thy word is a lamp unto my feet, and a light unto my path."

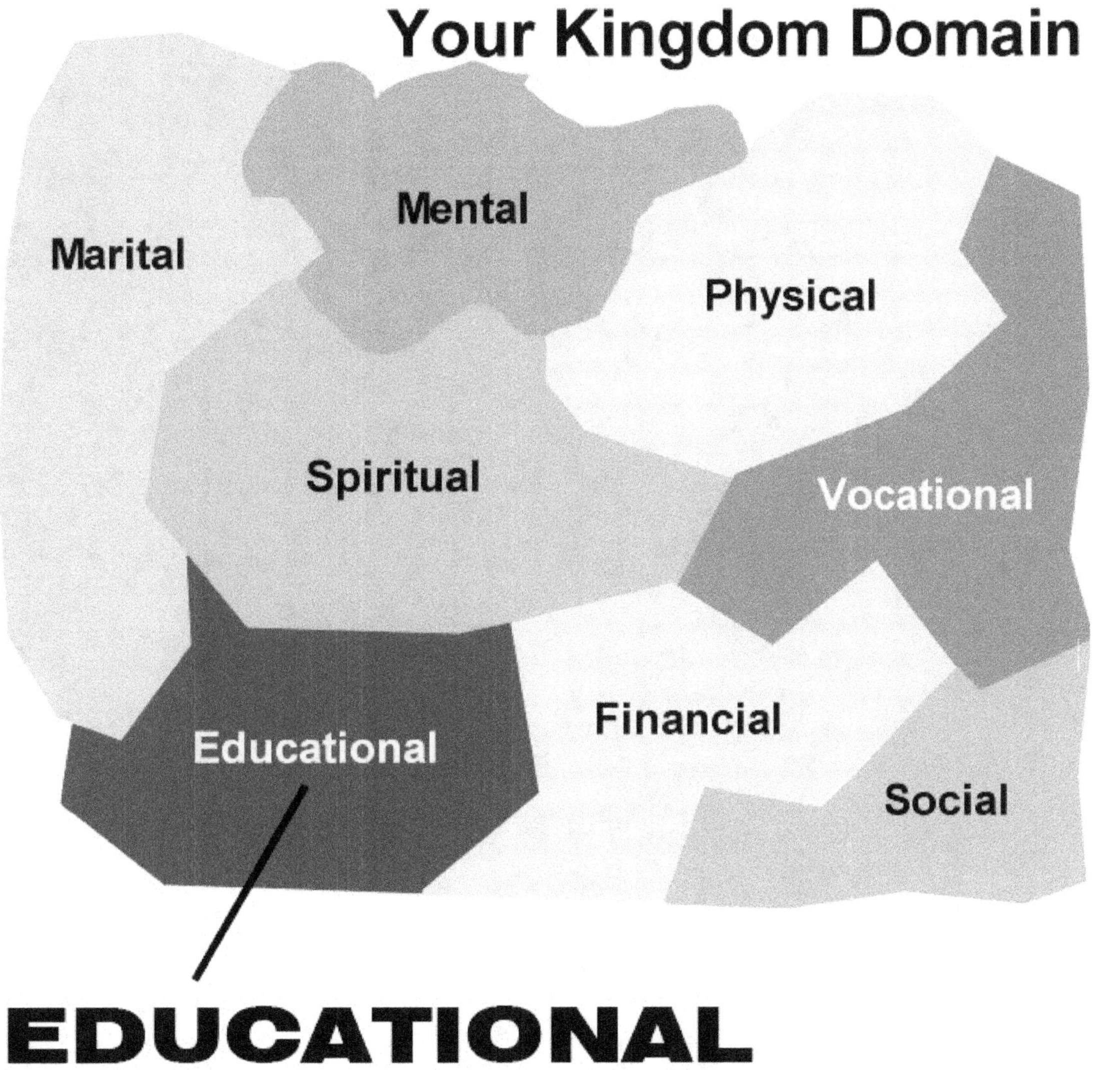

EDUCATIONAL – EDUCATIONAL – EDUCATIONAL - EDUCATIONAL

Your Kingdom Domain

- Marital
- Mental
- Physical
- Spiritual
- Vocational
- Educational
- Financial
- Social

EDUCATIONAL

© 2012 Mighty Eagle Publishing   All Rights Reserved
www.mightyeagle.com   www.doctordanieldaves.com

Prov. 16:2 (NIV) All a man's ways seem innocent to him, but motives are weighed by the LORD.

Keywords That may Help You With Your Goals: School, College, Degree, I.Q., G.P.A., Books, Seminar, Language, Professional, Masters, Doctoral, Study, Time Management, Coaching.

EDUCATIONAL GOALS: Short, Medium, Long Term

Create your target goals now. Modify them throughout the year as you walk through God's Word & daily meditation.

Short Term Goals – One Year Or Less   Date Created:_____

1._____

2._____

3._____

Medium Term Goals – Five Years   Date Created:_____

1._____

2._____

3._____

Long Term Goals – Ten Years   Date Created:_____

1._____

2._____

3._____

Long Term Goals – Twenty Years   Date Created:_____

1._____

2._____

3._____

Long Term Goals – Fifty Years   Date Created:_____

1._____

2._____

3._____

*Psalms 119:105 "Thy word is a lamp unto my feet, and a light unto my path."*_____

© 2012 Mighty Eagle Publishing   All Rights Reserved
www.mightyeagle.com   www.doctordanieldaves.com

EDUCATIONAL GOALS: Continued . . .

Notes:

Psalms 119:105 "Thy word is a lamp unto my feet, and a light unto my path."

© 2012 Mighty Eagle Publishing   All Rights Reserved
www.mightyeagle.com   www.doctordanieldaves.com

DAILY NOTES AND JOURNAL ENTRIES: *(Remember to date your journal entries)*

Habakkuk 2:2 "Write the vision, and make it plain upon tables, that he may run that readeth it."

DAILY NOTES AND JOURNAL ENTRIES: *(Remember to date your journal entries)*

Psalms 119:105 "*Thy word is a lamp unto my feet, and a light unto my path.*"

© 2012 Mighty Eagle Publishing   All Rights Reserved
www.mightyeagle.com   www.doctordanieldaves.com

DAILY NOTES AND JOURNAL ENTRIES: *(Remember to date your journal entries)*

Educational

Habakkuk 2:2 "Write the vision, and make it plain upon tables, that he may run that readeth it."

© 2012 Mighty Eagle Publishing   All Rights Reserved
www.mightyeagle.com   www.doctordanieldaves.com

DAILY NOTES AND JOURNAL ENTRIES: *(Remember to date your journal entries)*

Psalms 119:105 "Thy word is a lamp unto my feet, and a light unto my path."

© 2012 Mighty Eagle Publishing   All Rights Reserved
www.mightyeagle.com   www.doctordanieldaves.com

DAILY NOTES AND JOURNAL ENTRIES: *(Remember to date your journal entries)*

Habakkuk 2:2 "Write the vision, and make it plain upon tables, that he may run that readeth it."

© 2012 Mighty Eagle Publishing   All Rights Reserved
www.mightyeagle.com   www.doctordanieldaves.com

DAILY NOTES AND JOURNAL ENTRIES: *(Remember to date your journal entries)*

Psalms 119:105 "Thy word is a lamp unto my feet, and a light unto my path."

© 2012 Mighty Eagle Publishing   All Rights Reserved
www.mightyeagle.com   www.doctordanieldaves.com

DAILY NOTES AND JOURNAL ENTRIES: *(Remember to date your journal entries)*

Habakkuk 2:2 "Write the vision, and make it plain upon tables, that he may run that readeth it."

© 2012 Mighty Eagle Publishing   All Rights Reserved
www.mightyeagle.com   www.doctordanieldaves.com

DAILY NOTES AND JOURNAL ENTRIES: *(Remember to date your journal entries)*

Psalms 119:105 "Thy word is a lamp unto my feet, and a light unto my path."

© 2012 Mighty Eagle Publishing   All Rights Reserved
www.mightyeagle.com   www.doctordanieldaves.com

DAILY NOTES AND JOURNAL ENTRIES: *(Remember to date your journal entries)*

Habakkuk 2:2 "Write the vision, and make it plain upon tables, that he may run that readeth it."

© 2012 Mighty Eagle Publishing   All Rights Reserved
www.mightyeagle.com   www.doctordanieldaves.com

DAILY NOTES AND JOURNAL ENTRIES: *(Remember to date your journal entries)*

Psalms 119:105 "Thy word is a lamp unto my feet, and a light unto my path."

DAILY NOTES AND JOURNAL ENTRIES: *(Remember to date your journal entries)*

Habakkuk 2:2 "Write the vision, and make it plain upon tables, that he may run that readeth it."

© 2012 Mighty Eagle Publishing   All Rights Reserved
www.mightyeagle.com   www.doctordanieldaves.com

DAILY NOTES AND JOURNAL ENTRIES: *(Remember to date your journal entries)*

Psalms 119:105 "*Thy word is a lamp unto my feet, and a light unto my path.*"

© 2012 Mighty Eagle Publishing   All Rights Reserved
www.mightyeagle.com   www.doctordanieldaves.com

DAILY NOTES AND JOURNAL ENTRIES: *(Remember to date your journal entries)*

Educational

Habakkuk 2:2 "Write the vision, and make it plain upon tables, that he may run that readeth it."

© 2012 Mighty Eagle Publishing   All Rights Reserved
www.mightyeagle.com   www.doctordanieldaves.com

DAILY NOTES AND JOURNAL ENTRIES: *(Remember to date your journal entries)*

Psalms 119:105 "Thy word is a lamp unto my feet, and a light unto my path."

© 2012 Mighty Eagle Publishing   All Rights Reserved
www.mightyeagle.com   www.doctordanieldaves.com

DAILY NOTES AND JOURNAL ENTRIES: *(Remember to date your journal entries)*

Habakkuk 2:2 "Write the vision, and make it plain upon tables, that he may run that readeth it."

© 2012 Mighty Eagle Publishing   All Rights Reserved
www.mightyeagle.com   www.doctordanieldaves.com

DAILY NOTES AND JOURNAL ENTRIES: *(Remember to date your journal entries)*

Psalms 119:105 "Thy word is a lamp unto my feet, and a light unto my path."

© 2012 Mighty Eagle Publishing   All Rights Reserved
www.mightyeagle.com   www.doctordanieldaves.com

DAILY NOTES AND JOURNAL ENTRIES: *(Remember to date your journal entries)*

Habakkuk 2;2 "Write the vision, and make it plain upon tables, that he may run that readeth it."

© 2012 Mighty Eagle Publishing   All Rights Reserved
www.mightyeagle.com   www.doctordanieldaves.com

DAILY NOTES AND JOURNAL ENTRIES: *(Remember to date your journal entries)*

Psalms 119:105 "Thy word is a lamp unto my feet, and a light unto my path."

© 2012 Mighty Eagle Publishing   All Rights Reserved
www.mightyeagle.com   www.doctordanieldaves.com

DAILY NOTES AND JOURNAL ENTRIES: *(Remember to date your journal entries)*

Educational

Habakkuk 2:2 "Write the vision, and make it plain upon tables, that he may run that readeth it."

© 2012 Mighty Eagle Publishing   All Rights Reserved
www.mightyeagle.com   www.doctordanieldaves.com

DAILY NOTES AND JOURNAL ENTRIES: *(Remember to date your journal entries)*

Psalms 119:105 "Thy word is a lamp unto my feet, and a light unto my path."

© 2012 Mighty Eagle Publishing   All Rights Reserved
www.mightyeagle.com   www.doctordanieldaves.com

DAILY NOTES AND JOURNAL ENTRIES: *(Remember to date your journal entries)*

Educational

Habakkuk 2:2 "Write the vision, and make it plain upon tables, that he may run that readeth it."

© 2012 Mighty Eagle Publishing   All Rights Reserved
www.mightyeagle.com   www.doctordanieldaves.com

DAILY NOTES AND JOURNAL ENTRIES: *(Remember to date your journal entries)*

Psalms 119:105 "Thy word is a lamp unto my feet, and a light unto my path."

© 2012 Mighty Eagle Publishing All Rights Reserved
www.mightyeagle.com www.doctordanieldaves.com

DAILY NOTES AND JOURNAL ENTRIES: *(Remember to date your journal entries)*

Educational

Habakkuk 2:2 "*Write the vision, and make it plain upon tables, that he may run that readeth it.*"

© 2012 Mighty Eagle Publishing   All Rights Reserved
www.mightyeagle.com   www.doctordanieldaves.com

DAILY NOTES AND JOURNAL ENTRIES: *(Remember to date your journal entries)*

Psalms 119:105 "Thy word is a lamp unto my feet, and a light unto my path."

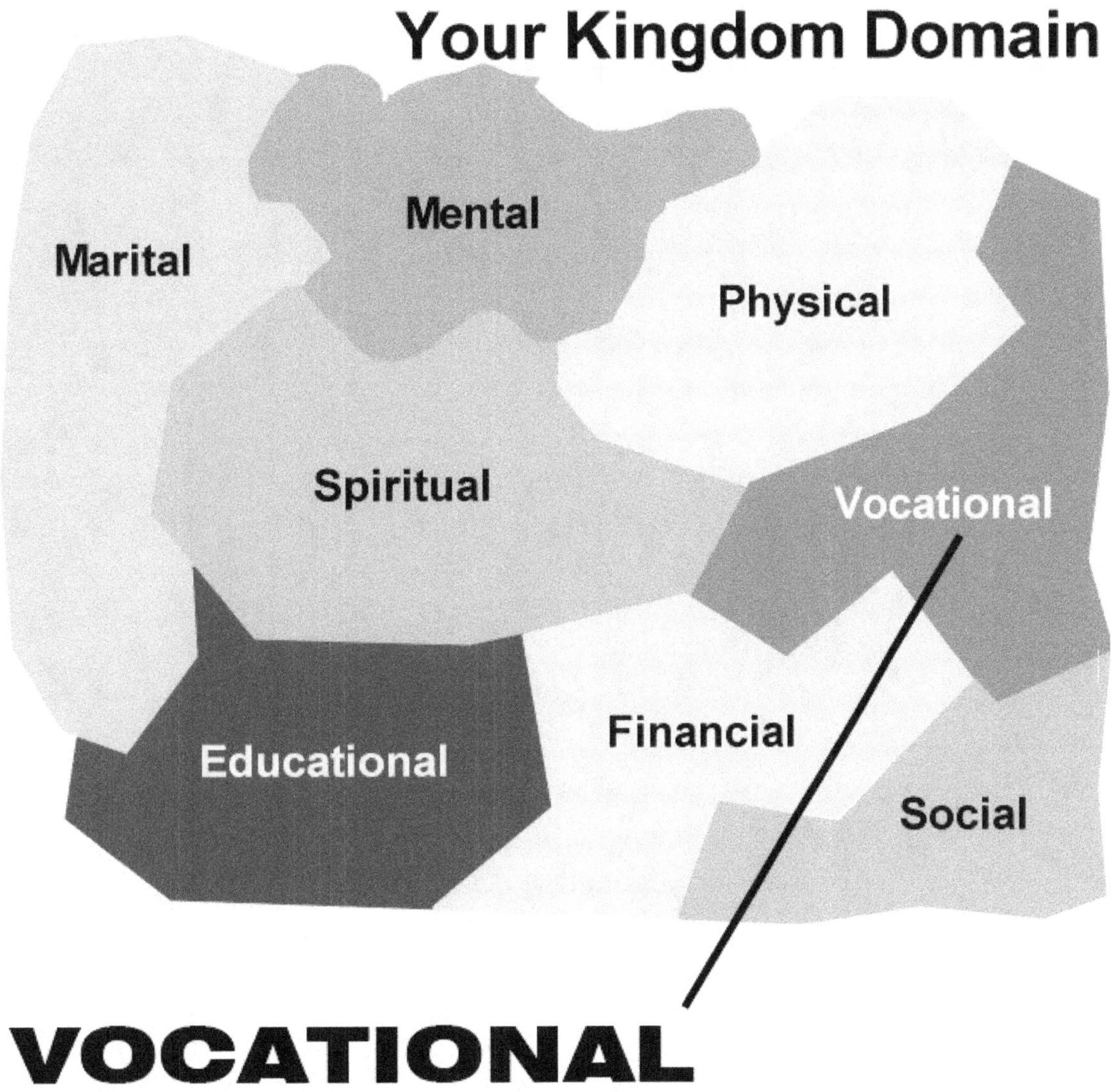

VOCATIONAL – VOCATIONAL – VOCATIONAL – VOCATIONAL

Your Kingdom Domain

Marital • Mental • Physical • Spiritual • Vocational • Educational • Financial • Social

VOCATIONAL

Prov. 16:1 (NIV) To man belong the plans of the heart, but from the LORD comes the reply of the tongue.

Keywords That may Help You With Your Goals: Job, Career, Occupation, Income, Work, Employment, Mission, Occupation, Profession, Assignment, Trade, Location, Calling, Duty, Undertaking.

VOCATIONAL GOALS: Short, Medium, Long Term

Create your target goals now. Modify them throughout the year as you walk through God's Word & daily meditation.

Short Term Goals – One Year Or Less   Date Created:_____

1._____

2._____

3._____

Medium Term Goals – Five Years   Date Created:_____

1._____

2._____

3._____

Long Term Goals – Ten Years   Date Created:_____

1._____

2._____

3._____

Long Term Goals – Twenty Years   Date Created:_____

1._____

2._____

3._____

Long Term Goals – Fifty Years   Date Created:_____

1._____

2._____

3._____

Psalms 119:105 "Thy word is a lamp unto my feet, and a light unto my path."

© 2012 Mighty Eagle Publishing   All Rights Reserved
www.mightyeagle.com   www.doctordanieldaves.com

VOCATIONAL GOALS: Continued . . .

Notes:_____

Psalms 119:105 "Thy word is a lamp unto my feet, and a light unto my path."

DAILY NOTES AND JOURNAL ENTRIES: *(Remember to date your journal entries)*

Vocational

Habakkuk 2:2 "Write the vision, and make it plain upon tables, that he may run that readeth it."

© 2012 Mighty Eagle Publishing   All Rights Reserved
www.mightyeagle.com   www.doctordanieldaves.com

DAILY NOTES AND JOURNAL ENTRIES: *(Remember to date your journal entries)*

Psalms 119:105 "Thy word is a lamp unto my feet, and a light unto my path."

DAILY NOTES AND JOURNAL ENTRIES: *(Remember to date your journal entries)*

Vocational

Habakkuk 2:2 "Write the vision, and make it plain upon tables, that he may run that readeth it."

© 2012 Mighty Eagle Publishing   All Rights Reserved
www.mightyeagle.com   www.doctordanieldaves.com

DAILY NOTES AND JOURNAL ENTRIES: *(Remember to date your journal entries)*

Psalms 119:105 "*Thy word is a lamp unto my feet, and a light unto my path.*"

© 2012 Mighty Eagle Publishing   All Rights Reserved
www.mightyeagle.com   www.doctordanieldaves.com

DAILY NOTES AND JOURNAL ENTRIES: *(Remember to date your journal entries)*

Vocational

Habakkuk 2:2 "Write the vision, and make it plain upon tables, that he may run that readeth it."

© 2012 Mighty Eagle Publishing   All Rights Reserved
www.mightyeagle.com   www.doctordanieldaves.com

DAILY NOTES AND JOURNAL ENTRIES: *(Remember to date your journal entries)*

Psalms 119:105 "Thy word is a lamp unto my feet, and a light unto my path."

DAILY NOTES AND JOURNAL ENTRIES: *(Remember to date your journal entries)*

Vocational

Habakkuk 2:2 "Write the vision, and make it plain upon tables, that he may run that readeth it."

© 2012 Mighty Eagle Publishing   All Rights Reserved
www.mightyeagle.com   www.doctordanieldaves.com

DAILY NOTES AND JOURNAL ENTRIES: *(Remember to date your journal entries)*

Psalms 119:105 "Thy word is a lamp unto my feet, and a light unto my path."

DAILY NOTES AND JOURNAL ENTRIES: *(Remember to date your journal entries)*

Vocational

Habakkuk 2:2 "Write the vision, and make it plain upon tables, that he may run that readeth it."

DAILY NOTES AND JOURNAL ENTRIES: *(Remember to date your journal entries)*

Psalms 119:105 "Thy word is a lamp unto my feet, and a light unto my path."

DAILY NOTES AND JOURNAL ENTRIES: *(Remember to date your journal entries)*

Vocational

Habakkuk 2:2 "Write the vision, and make it plain upon tables, that he may run that readeth it."

© 2012 Mighty Eagle Publishing   All Rights Reserved
www.mightyeagle.com   www.doctordanieldaves.com

DAILY NOTES AND JOURNAL ENTRIES: *(Remember to date your journal entries)*

Psalms 119:105 "Thy word is a lamp unto my feet, and a light unto my path."

© 2012 Mighty Eagle Publishing   All Rights Reserved
www.mightyeagle.com   www.doctordanieldaves.com

DAILY NOTES AND JOURNAL ENTRIES: *(Remember to date your journal entries)*

Vocational

Habakkuk 2:2 "Write the vision, and make it plain upon tables, that he may run that readeth it."

© 2012 Mighty Eagle Publishing   All Rights Reserved
www.mightyeagle.com   www.doctordanieldaves.com

DAILY NOTES AND JOURNAL ENTRIES: *(Remember to date your journal entries)*

Psalms 119:105 "Thy word is a lamp unto my feet, and a light unto my path."

DAILY NOTES AND JOURNAL ENTRIES: *(Remember to date your journal entries)*

Vocational

Habakkuk 2:2 "Write the vision, and make it plain upon tables, that he may run that readeth it."

© 2012 Mighty Eagle Publishing   All Rights Reserved
www.mightyeagle.com   www.doctordanieldaves.com

DAILY NOTES AND JOURNAL ENTRIES: *(Remember to date your journal entries)*

Psalms 119:105 "Thy word is a lamp unto my feet, and a light unto my path."

© 2012 Mighty Eagle Publishing   All Rights Reserved
www.mightyeagle.com   www.doctordanieldaves.com

DAILY NOTES AND JOURNAL ENTRIES: *(Remember to date your journal entries)*

Habakkuk 2:2 "Write the vision, and make it plain upon tables, that he may run that readeth it."

© 2012 Mighty Eagle Publishing   All Rights Reserved
www.mightyeagle.com   www.doctordanieldaves.com

DAILY NOTES AND JOURNAL ENTRIES: *(Remember to date your journal entries)*

Psalms 119:105 "Thy word is a lamp unto my feet, and a light unto my path."

© 2012 Mighty Eagle Publishing   All Rights Reserved
www.mightyeagle.com   www.doctordanieldaves.com

DAILY NOTES AND JOURNAL ENTRIES: *(Remember to date your journal entries)*

Vocational

Habakkuk 2:2 "Write the vision, and make it plain upon tables, that he may run that readeth it."

© 2012 Mighty Eagle Publishing   All Rights Reserved
www.mightyeagle.com   www.doctordanieldaves.com

DAILY NOTES AND JOURNAL ENTRIES: *(Remember to date your journal entries)*

Psalms 119:105 "Thy word is a lamp unto my feet, and a light unto my path."

© 2012 Mighty Eagle Publishing   All Rights Reserved
www.mightyeagle.com   www.doctordanieldaves.com

DAILY NOTES AND JOURNAL ENTRIES: *(Remember to date your journal entries)*

Vocational

Habakkuk 2:2 "Write the vision, and make it plain upon tables, that he may run that readeth it."

© 2012 Mighty Eagle Publishing   All Rights Reserved
www.mightyeagle.com   www.doctordanieldaves.com

DAILY NOTES AND JOURNAL ENTRIES: *(Remember to date your journal entries)*

Psalms 119:105 "*Thy word is a lamp unto my feet, and a light unto my path.*"

DAILY NOTES AND JOURNAL ENTRIES: *(Remember to date your journal entries)*

Vocational

Habakkuk 2:2 "Write the vision, and make it plain upon tables, that he may run that readeth it."

© 2012 Mighty Eagle Publishing   All Rights Reserved
www.mightyeagle.com   www.doctordanieldaves.com

DAILY NOTES AND JOURNAL ENTRIES: *(Remember to date your journal entries)*

Psalms 119:105 "Thy word is a lamp unto my feet, and a light unto my path."

© 2012 Mighty Eagle Publishing   All Rights Reserved
www.mightyeagle.com   www.doctordanieldaves.com

Marital

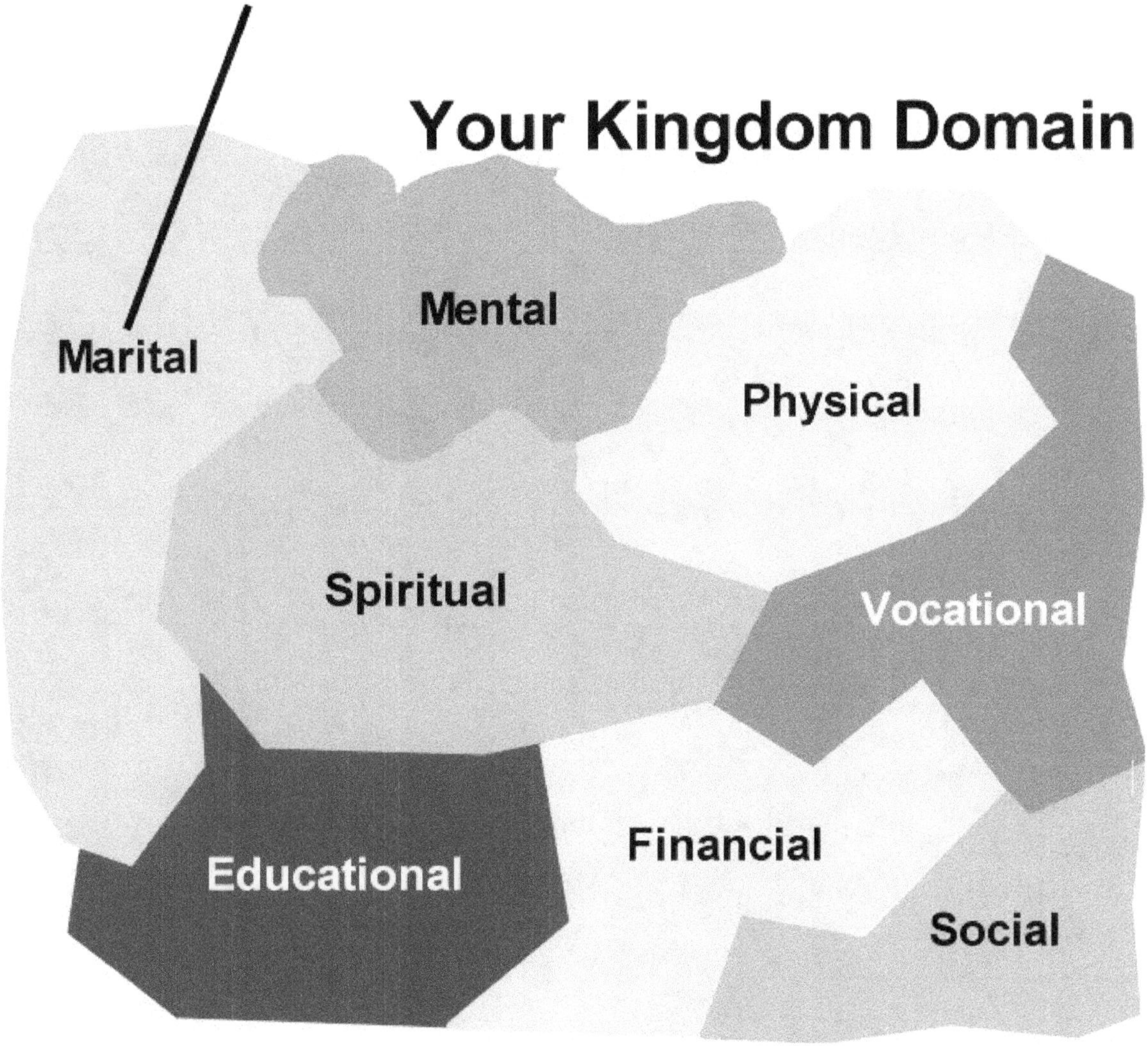

Your Kingdom Domain

- Marital
- Mental
- Physical
- Spiritual
- Vocational
- Educational
- Financial
- Social

© 2012 Mighty Eagle Publishing   All Rights Reserved
www.mightyeagle.com   www.doctordanieldaves.com

Psalms 37:4-6 (NIV) Delight yourself in the LORD and he will give you the desires of your heart. Commit your way to the LORD; trust in him and he will do this: He will make your righteousness shine like the dawn, the justice of your cause like the noonday sun.

Keywords That may Help You With Your Goals: Union, Wedlock, Counsel, Partner, Match, Dating, Standards, Morals, Sacrifice, Submission, Love, Tie, Commitment, Vow, Wedding. Unity, Oneness, Strength, Fulfillment, Giving

MARITAL GOALS: Short, Medium, Long Term

Create your target goals now. Modify them throughout the year as you walk through God's Word & daily meditation.

Short Term Goals – One Year Or Less   Date Created:_____

1._____
2._____
3._____

Medium Term Goals – Five Years   Date Created:_____

1._____
2._____
3._____

Long Term Goals – Ten Years   Date Created:_____

1._____
2._____
3._____

Long Term Goals – Twenty Years   Date Created:_____

1._____
2._____
3._____

Long Term Goals – Fifty Years   Date Created:_____

1._____
2._____
3._____

*Psalms 119:105 "Thy word is a lamp unto my feet, and a light unto my path."*_____

© 2012 Mighty Eagle Publishing   All Rights Reserved
www.mightyeagle.com   www.doctordanieldaves.com

MARITAL GOALS: Continued . . .

Notes: _____

Goals *Marital*

Psalms 119:105 "Thy word is a lamp unto my feet, and a light unto my path."

© 2012 Mighty Eagle Publishing   All Rights Reserved
www.mightyeagle.com   www.doctordanieldaves.com

DAILY NOTES AND JOURNAL ENTRIES: *(Remember to date your journal entries)*

Habakkuk 2:2 "Write the vision, and make it plain upon tables, that he may run that readeth it."

© 2012 Mighty Eagle Publishing   All Rights Reserved
www.mightyeagle.com   www.doctordanieldaves.com

Marital

DAILY NOTES AND JOURNAL ENTRIES: *(Remember to date your journal entries)*

Psalms 119:105 "Thy word is a lamp unto my feet, and a light unto my path."

DAILY NOTES AND JOURNAL ENTRIES: *(Remember to date your journal entries)*

Marital

Habakkuk 2:2 "Write the vision, and make it plain upon tables, that he may run that readeth it."

© 2012 Mighty Eagle Publishing   All Rights Reserved
www.mightyeagle.com   www.doctordanieldaves.com

DAILY NOTES AND JOURNAL ENTRIES: *(Remember to date your journal entries)*

Psalms 119:105 "*Thy word is a lamp unto my feet, and a light unto my path.*"

© 2012 Mighty Eagle Publishing   All Rights Reserved
www.mightyeagle.com   www.doctordanieldaves.com

DAILY NOTES AND JOURNAL ENTRIES: *(Remember to date your journal entries)*

Marital

Habakkuk 2:2 "Write the vision, and make it plain upon tables, that he may run that readeth it."

© 2012 Mighty Eagle Publishing   All Rights Reserved
www.mightyeagle.com   www.doctordanieldaves.com

DAILY NOTES AND JOURNAL ENTRIES: *(Remember to date your journal entries)*

Psalms 119:105 "Thy word is a lamp unto my feet, and a light unto my path."

DAILY NOTES AND JOURNAL ENTRIES: *(Remember to date your journal entries)*

Marital

Habakkuk 2:2 "Write the vision, and make it plain upon tables, that he may run that readeth it."

© 2012 Mighty Eagle Publishing   All Rights Reserved
www.mightyeagle.com   www.doctordanieldaves.com

DAILY NOTES AND JOURNAL ENTRIES: *(Remember to date your journal entries)*

Psalms 119:105 "*Thy word is a lamp unto my feet, and a light unto my path.*"

© 2012 Mighty Eagle Publishing   All Rights Reserved
www.mightyeagle.com   www.doctordanieldaves.com

DAILY NOTES AND JOURNAL ENTRIES: *(Remember to date your journal entries)*

Marital

Habakkuk 2:2 "Write the vision, and make it plain upon tables, that he may run that readeth it."

© 2012 Mighty Eagle Publishing   All Rights Reserved
www.mightyeagle.com   www.doctordanieldaves.com

DAILY NOTES AND JOURNAL ENTRIES: *(Remember to date your journal entries)*

Psalms 119:105 "Thy word is a lamp unto my feet, and a light unto my path."

© 2012 Mighty Eagle Publishing   All Rights Reserved
www.mightyeagle.com   www.doctordanieldaves.com

DAILY NOTES AND JOURNAL ENTRIES: *(Remember to date your journal entries)*

Marital

Habakkuk 2:2 "Write the vision, and make it plain upon tables, that he may run that readeth it."

© 2012 Mighty Eagle Publishing   All Rights Reserved
www.mightyeagle.com   www.doctordanieldaves.com

DAILY NOTES AND JOURNAL ENTRIES: *(Remember to date your journal entries)*

Psalms 119:105 "Thy word is a lamp unto my feet, and a light unto my path."

DAILY NOTES AND JOURNAL ENTRIES: *(Remember to date your journal entries)*

Marital

Habakkuk 2:2 "Write the vision, and make it plain upon tables, that he may run that readeth it."

© 2012 Mighty Eagle Publishing   All Rights Reserved
www.mightyeagle.com   www.doctordanieldaves.com

DAILY NOTES AND JOURNAL ENTRIES: *(Remember to date your journal entries)*

Psalms 119:105 "Thy word is a lamp unto my feet, and a light unto my path."

© 2012 Mighty Eagle Publishing   All Rights Reserved
www.mightyeagle.com   www.doctordanieldaves.com

DAILY NOTES AND JOURNAL ENTRIES: *(Remember to date your journal entries)*

Marital

Habakkuk 2:2 "Write the vision, and make it plain upon tables, that he may run that readeth it."

© 2012 Mighty Eagle Publishing   All Rights Reserved
www.mightyeagle.com   www.doctordanieldaves.com

DAILY NOTES AND JOURNAL ENTRIES: *(Remember to date your journal entries)*

Psalms 119:105 "Thy word is a lamp unto my feet, and a light unto my path."

© 2012 Mighty Eagle Publishing   All Rights Reserved
www.mightyeagle.com   www.doctordanieldaves.com

DAILY NOTES AND JOURNAL ENTRIES: *(Remember to date your journal entries)*

Habakkuk 2:2 "Write the vision, and make it plain upon tables, that he may run that readeth it."

© 2012 Mighty Eagle Publishing   All Rights Reserved
www.mightyeagle.com   www.doctordanieldaves.com

DAILY NOTES AND JOURNAL ENTRIES: *(Remember to date your journal entries)*

Psalms 119:105 "Thy word is a lamp unto my feet, and a light unto my path."

© 2012 Mighty Eagle Publishing   All Rights Reserved
www.mightyeagle.com   www.doctordanieldaves.com

DAILY NOTES AND JOURNAL ENTRIES: *(Remember to date your journal entries)*

Marital

Habakkuk 2:2 "Write the vision, and make it plain upon tables, that he may run that readeth it."

© 2012 Mighty Eagle Publishing   All Rights Reserved
www.mightyeagle.com   www.doctordanieldaves.com

DAILY NOTES AND JOURNAL ENTRIES: *(Remember to date your journal entries)*

Psalms 119:105 "Thy word is a lamp unto my feet, and a light unto my path."

DAILY NOTES AND JOURNAL ENTRIES: *(Remember to date your journal entries)*

Habakkuk 2:2 "Write the vision, and make it plain upon tables, that he may run that readeth it."

© 2012 Mighty Eagle Publishing   All Rights Reserved
www.mightyeagle.com   www.doctordanieldaves.com

Marital

DAILY NOTES AND JOURNAL ENTRIES: *(Remember to date your journal entries)*

Psalms 119:105 "Thy word is a lamp unto my feet, and a light unto my path."

© 2012 Mighty Eagle Publishing   All Rights Reserved
www.mightyeagle.com   www.doctordanieldaves.com

DAILY NOTES AND JOURNAL ENTRIES: *(Remember to date your journal entries)*

Marital

Habakkuk 2:2 "*Write the vision, and make it plain upon tables, that he may run that readeth it.*"

© 2012 Mighty Eagle Publishing   All Rights Reserved
www.mightyeagle.com   www.doctordanieldaves.com

DAILY NOTES AND JOURNAL ENTRIES: *(Remember to date your journal entries)*

Psalms 119:105 "*Thy word is a lamp unto my feet, and a light unto my path.*"

© 2012 Mighty Eagle Publishing   All Rights Reserved
www.mightyeagle.com   www.doctordanieldaves.com

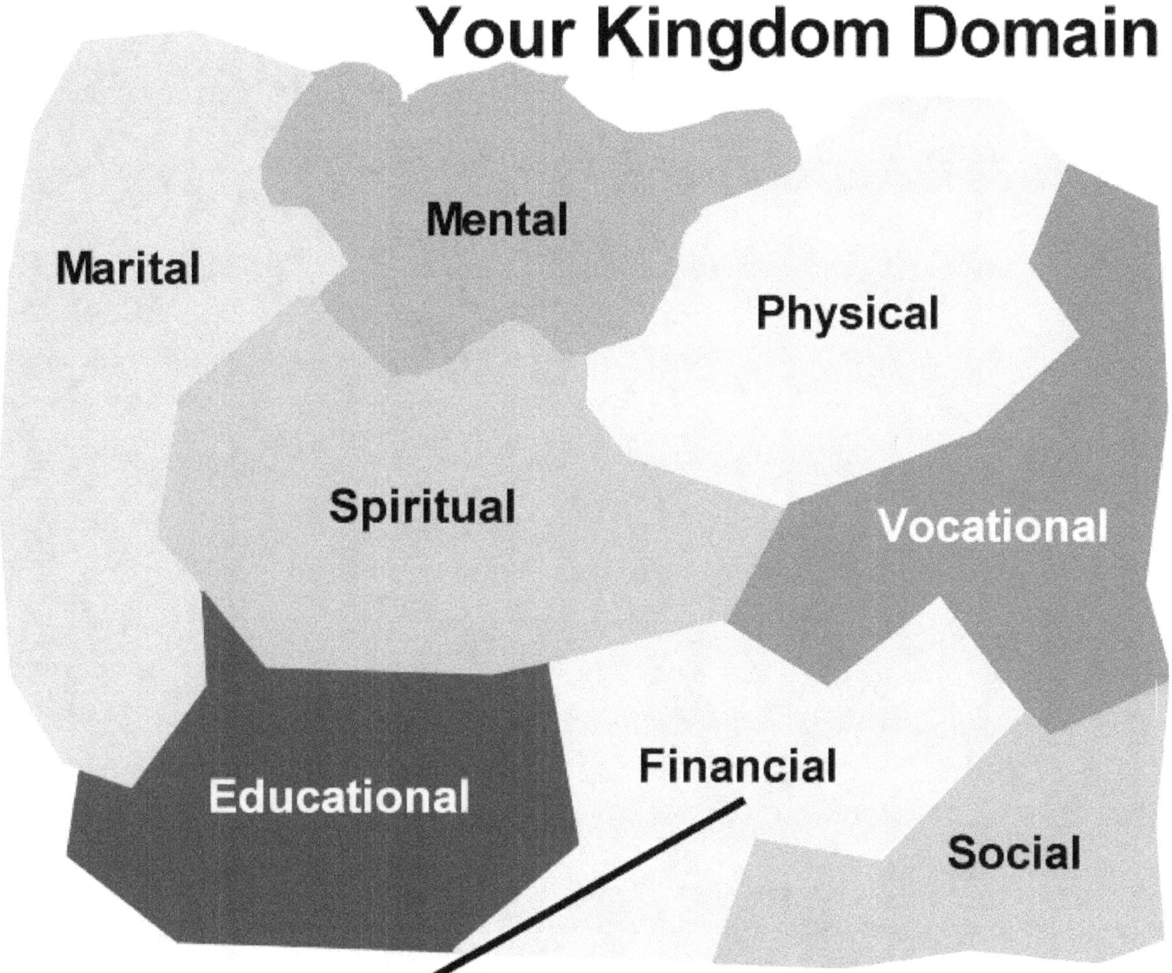

FINANCIAL – FINANCIAL – FINANCIAL – FINANCIAL

Your Kingdom Domain

Marital · Mental · Physical · Spiritual · Vocational · Educational · Financial · Social

FINANCIAL

© 2012 Mighty Eagle Publishing   All Rights Reserved
www.mightyeagle.com   www.doctordanieldaves.com

Prov. 13:22 (KJV) A good man leaveth an inheritance to his children's children: and the wealth of the sinner is laid up for the just.

Keywords That may Help You With Your Goals: Money, Savings, Portfolio, Financial Education, Budget, Banking, Loans, Self Control, Tithe, Offerings, Giving, Widows, Orphans, Needy, Economics, Investment, Business, Management, Commerce, Inventions, Retirement, Wealth, Royalty, Reward, Award. Streams Of Income, Freedom, Time Management

"When you establish your financial goals, most of your future decisions about money will have already been made."

– Gene Strite, Author
www.genestrite.com

FINANCIAL GOALS: Short, Medium, Long Term

Create your target goals now. Modify them throughout the year as you walk through God's Word & daily meditation.

Short Term Goals – One Year Or Less   Date Created:_____

1._____

2._____

3._____

Medium Term Goals – Five Years   Date Created:_____

1._____

2._____

3._____

Long Term Goals – Ten Years   Date Created:_____

1._____

2._____

3._____

Long Term Goals – Twenty Years   Date Created:_____

1._____

2._____

3._____

Long Term Goals – Fifty Years   Date Created:_____

1._____

2._____

3._____

Psalms 119:105 "Thy word is a lamp unto my feet, and a light unto my path."

© 2012 Mighty Eagle Publishing   All Rights Reserved
www.mightyeagle.com   www.doctordanieldaves.com

FINANCIAL GOALS: Continued . . .

Notes:

Psalms 119:105 "Thy word is a lamp unto my feet, and a light unto my path."

© 2012 Mighty Eagle Publishing   All Rights Reserved
www.mightyeagle.com   www.doctordanieldaves.com

DAILY NOTES AND JOURNAL ENTRIES: *(Remember to date your journal entries)*

Habakkuk 2:2 "Write the vision, and make it plain upon tables, that he may run that readeth it."

© 2012 Mighty Eagle Publishing   All Rights Reserved
www.mightyeagle.com   www.doctordanieldaves.com

Financial

DAILY NOTES AND JOURNAL ENTRIES: *(Remember to date your journal entries)*

Psalms 119:105 "Thy word is a lamp unto my feet, and a light unto my path."

DAILY NOTES AND JOURNAL ENTRIES: *(Remember to date your journal entries)*

Habakkuk 2:2 "Write the vision, and make it plain upon tables, that he may run that readeth it."

© 2012 Mighty Eagle Publishing   All Rights Reserved
www.mightyeagle.com   www.doctordanieldaves.com

Financial

DAILY NOTES AND JOURNAL ENTRIES: *(Remember to date your journal entries)*

Psalms 119:105 "Thy word is a lamp unto my feet, and a light unto my path."

DAILY NOTES AND JOURNAL ENTRIES: *(Remember to date your journal entries)*

Habakkuk 2:2 "Write the vision, and make it plain upon tables, that he may run that readeth it."

DAILY NOTES AND JOURNAL ENTRIES: *(Remember to date your journal entries)*

Psalms 119:105 "Thy word is a lamp unto my feet, and a light unto my path."

DAILY NOTES AND JOURNAL ENTRIES: *(Remember to date your journal entries)*

Habakkuk 2:2 "Write the vision, and make it plain upon tables, that he may run that readeth it."

DAILY NOTES AND JOURNAL ENTRIES: *(Remember to date your journal entries)*

Psalms 119:105 "Thy word is a lamp unto my feet, and a light unto my path."

DAILY NOTES AND JOURNAL ENTRIES: *(Remember to date your journal entries)*

Habakkuk 2:2 "Write the vision, and make it plain upon tables, that he may run that readeth it."

© 2012 Mighty Eagle Publishing   All Rights Reserved
www.mightyeagle.com   www.doctordanieldaves.com

Financial

DAILY NOTES AND JOURNAL ENTRIES: *(Remember to date your journal entries)*

Psalms 119:105 "Thy word is a lamp unto my feet, and a light unto my path."

© 2012 Mighty Eagle Publishing   All Rights Reserved
www.mightyeagle.com   www.doctordanieldaves.com

DAILY NOTES AND JOURNAL ENTRIES: *(Remember to date your journal entries)*

Habakkuk 2:2 "Write the vision, and make it plain upon tables, that he may run that readeth it."

© 2012 Mighty Eagle Publishing   All Rights Reserved
www.mightyeagle.com   www.doctordanieldaves.com

Financial

DAILY NOTES AND JOURNAL ENTRIES: *(Remember to date your journal entries)*

Psalms 119:105 "Thy word is a lamp unto my feet, and a light unto my path."

DAILY NOTES AND JOURNAL ENTRIES: *(Remember to date your journal entries)*

Habakkuk 2:2 "Write the vision, and make it plain upon tables, that he may run that readeth it."

DAILY NOTES AND JOURNAL ENTRIES: *(Remember to date your journal entries)*

Psalms 119:105 "Thy word is a lamp unto my feet, and a light unto my path."

© 2012 Mighty Eagle Publishing   All Rights Reserved
www.mightyeagle.com   www.doctordanieldaves.com

DAILY NOTES AND JOURNAL ENTRIES: *(Remember to date your journal entries)*

Habakkuk 2:2 "Write the vision, and make it plain upon tables, that he may run that readeth it."

DAILY NOTES AND JOURNAL ENTRIES: *(Remember to date your journal entries)*

Psalms 119:105 "Thy word is a lamp unto my feet, and a light unto my path."

© 2012 Mighty Eagle Publishing   All Rights Reserved
www.mightyeagle.com   www.doctordanieldaves.com

DAILY NOTES AND JOURNAL ENTRIES: *(Remember to date your journal entries)*

Habakkuk 2:2 "Write the vision, and make it plain upon tables, that he may run that readeth it."

© 2012 Mighty Eagle Publishing   All Rights Reserved
www.mightyeagle.com   www.doctordanieldaves.com

DAILY NOTES AND JOURNAL ENTRIES: *(Remember to date your journal entries)*

Psalms 119:105 "Thy word is a lamp unto my feet, and a light unto my path."

DAILY NOTES AND JOURNAL ENTRIES: *(Remember to date your journal entries)*

Habakkuk 2:2 "Write the vision, and make it plain upon tables, that he may run that readeth it."

DAILY NOTES AND JOURNAL ENTRIES: *(Remember to date your journal entries)*

Psalms 119:105 *"Thy word is a lamp unto my feet, and a light unto my path."*

DAILY NOTES AND JOURNAL ENTRIES: *(Remember to date your journal entries)*

Habakkuk 2:2 "Write the vision, and make it plain upon tables, that he may run that readeth it."

© 2012 Mighty Eagle Publishing   All Rights Reserved
www.mightyeagle.com   www.doctordanieldaves.com

Financial

DAILY NOTES AND JOURNAL ENTRIES: *(Remember to date your journal entries)*

Psalms 119:105 "Thy word is a lamp unto my feet, and a light unto my path."

© 2012 Mighty Eagle Publishing   All Rights Reserved
www.mightyeagle.com   www.doctordanieldaves.com

DAILY NOTES AND JOURNAL ENTRIES: *(Remember to date your journal entries)*

Habakkuk 2:2 "Write the vision, and make it plain upon tables, that he may run that readeth it."

© 2012 Mighty Eagle Publishing   All Rights Reserved
www.mightyeagle.com   www.doctordanieldaves.com

DAILY NOTES AND JOURNAL ENTRIES: *(Remember to date your journal entries)*

Psalms 119:105 *"Thy word is a lamp unto my feet, and a light unto my path."*

TWENTY FIVE WORD FOCUSED CORE LIFE STATEMENT

Directions: Write your twenty five word core life statement in this section using twenty five words or less. Do not go over twenty five words. Group all of your short, medium and long term goals, and focus on one statement of purpose. Use each word wisely. These are the twenty five words that you would use to explain to people who you are and what you do. You are defining who you are at the center core of your life, using powerful words. This core life statement will be the central driving force of your life. You may modify if from time to time. However, you must keep this statement of purpose before you every day and week of your life. Copy it on paper. Paste it on your refrigerator. Put it on the dashboard of your car. Tape it to your computer monitor screen. Then live it. Give quality time to it. Memorize it. Then activate it.

First Determination: Focused "Core Life Statement" In 25 Words

Modified Determination: Focused "Core Life Statement" In 25 Words

© 2012 Mighty Eagle Publishing   All Rights Reserved
www.mightyeagle.com   www.doctordanieldaves.com

DAILY GOAL CHECKLIST: *(Things To Do Today To Head Towards Goal Completion)*

Personal Meditation Scripture Of The Day: _____
_____

Goals To Accomplish Today:

1. _____
_____

2. _____
_____

3. _____
_____

4. _____
_____

5. _____
_____

6. _____
_____

7. _____
_____

8. _____
_____

9. _____
_____

10. _____
_____

Don't forget to visit www.doctordanieldaves.com and visit the Compass Guide Forum for daily inspiration and to post your own comments for others to read.

MAKE COPIES OF THIS PAGE FOR DAILY USE

© 2012 Mighty Eagle Publishing   All Rights Reserved
www.mightyeagle.com   www.doctordanieldaves.com

DAILY GOAL CHECKLIST: *(Things To Do Today To Head Towards Goal Completion)*

Personal Meditation Scripture Of The Day: _____
_____

Goals To Accomplish Today:

1. _____
_____

2. _____
_____

3. _____
_____

4. _____
_____

5. _____
_____

6. _____
_____

7. _____
_____

8. _____
_____

9. _____
_____

10. _____
_____

Don't forget to visit www.doctordanieldaves.com and visit the Compass Guide Forum for daily inspiration and to post your own comments for others to read.

MAKE COPIES OF THIS PAGE FOR DAILY USE

© 2012 Mighty Eagle Publishing   All Rights Reserved
www.mightyeagle.com   www.doctordanieldaves.com

DAILY GOAL CHECKLIST: (Things To Do Today To Head Towards Goal Completion)

Personal Meditation Scripture Of The Day: _____
_____

Goals To Accomplish Today:

1. _____
_____

2. _____
_____

3. _____
_____

4. _____
_____

5. _____
_____

6. _____
_____

7. _____
_____

8. _____
_____

9. _____
_____

10. _____
_____

Don't forget to visit www.doctordanieldaves.com and visit the Compass Guide Forum for daily inspiration and to post your own comments for others to read.

MAKE COPIES OF THIS PAGE FOR DAILY USE

© 2012 Mighty Eagle Publishing   All Rights Reserved
www.mightyeagle.com   www.doctordanieldaves.com

DAILY GOAL CHECKLIST: *(Things To Do Today To Head Towards Goal Completion)*

Personal Meditation Scripture Of The Day:_____

_____

Goals To Accomplish Today:

1. _____
   _____

2. _____
   _____

3. _____
   _____

4. _____
   _____

5. _____
   _____

6. _____
   _____

7. _____
   _____

8. _____
   _____

9. _____
   _____

10. _____
    _____

Don't forget to visit www.doctordanieldaves.com and visit the Compass Guide Forum for daily inspiration and to post your own comments for others to read.

MAKE COPIES OF THIS PAGE FOR DAILY USE

© 2012 Mighty Eagle Publishing   All Rights Reserved
www.mightyeagle.com   www.doctordanieldaves.com

DAILY GOAL CHECKLIST: *(Things To Do Today To Head Towards Goal Completion)*

Personal Meditation Scripture Of The Day:_____
_____

Goals To Accomplish Today:

1. _____
   _____
2. _____
   _____
3. _____
   _____
4. _____
   _____
5. _____
   _____
6. _____
   _____
7. _____
   _____
8. _____
   _____
9. _____
   _____
10. _____
    _____

Don't forget to visit www.doctordanieldaves.com and visit the Compass Guide Forum for daily inspiration and to post your own comments for others to read.

MAKE COPIES OF THIS PAGE FOR DAILY USE

© 2012 Mighty Eagle Publishing   All Rights Reserved
www.mightyeagle.com   www.doctordanieldaves.com

DAILY GOAL CHECKLIST: *(Things To Do Today To Head Towards Goal Completion)*

Personal Meditation Scripture Of The Day: _____

_____

Goals To Accomplish Today:

1. _____

2. _____

3. _____

4. _____

5. _____

6. _____

7. _____

8. _____

9. _____

10. _____

Don't forget to visit www.doctordanieldaves.com and visit the Compass Guide Forum for daily inspiration and to post your own comments for others to read.

MAKE COPIES OF THIS PAGE FOR DAILY USE

© 2012 Mighty Eagle Publishing   All Rights Reserved
www.mightyeagle.com   www.doctordanieldaves.com

DAILY GOAL CHECKLIST: (Things To Do Today To Head Towards Goal Completion)

Personal Meditation Scripture Of The Day: _____
_____

Goals To Accomplish Today:

1. _____
   _____

2. _____
   _____

3. _____
   _____

4. _____
   _____

5. _____
   _____

6. _____
   _____

7. _____
   _____

8. _____
   _____

9. _____
   _____

10. _____
    _____

Don't forget to visit www.doctordanieldaves.com and visit the Compass Guide Forum for daily inspiration and to post your own comments for others to read.

MAKE COPIES OF THIS PAGE FOR DAILY USE

© 2012 Mighty Eagle Publishing   All Rights Reserved
www.mightyeagle.com   www.doctordanieldaves.com

ADDITIONAL NOTES: *(Remember to date your journal entries)*

Habakkuk 2:2 "Write the vision, and make it plain upon tables, that he may run that readeth it."

© 2012 Mighty Eagle Publishing   All Rights Reserved
www.mightyeagle.com   www.doctordanieldaves.com

ADDITIONAL NOTES: *(Remember to date your journal entries)*

Habakkuk 2:2 "Write the vision, and make it plain upon tables, that he may run that readeth it."

ADDITIONAL NOTES: *(Remember to date your journal entries)*

Habakkuk 2:2 "Write the vision, and make it plain upon tables, that he may run that readeth it."

ADDITIONAL NOTES: *(Remember to date your journal entries)*

Habakkuk 2:2 "Write the vision, and make it plain upon tables, that he may run that readeth it."

ADDITIONAL NOTES: *(Remember to date your journal entries)*

Habakkuk 2:2 "Write the vision, and make it plain upon tables, that he may run that readeth it."

ADDITIONAL NOTES: *(Remember to date your journal entries)*

Habakkuk 2:2 "Write the vision, and make it plain upon tables, that he may run that readeth it."

ADDITIONAL NOTES: *(Remember to date your journal entries)*

Habakkuk 2:2 "Write the vision, and make it plain upon tables, that he may run that readeth it."

ADDITIONAL NOTES: *(Remember to date your journal entries)*

Habakkuk 2:2 "Write the vision, and make it plain upon tables, that he may run that readeth it."

ADDITIONAL NOTES: *(Remember to date your journal entries)*

Habakkuk 2:2 "Write the vision, and make it plain upon tables, that he may run that readeth it."

ADDITIONAL NOTES: *(Remember to date your journal entries)*

Habakkuk 2:2 "Write the vision, and make it plain upon tables, that he may run that readeth it."

www.ingramcontent.com/pod-product-compliance
Lightning Source LLC
Chambersburg PA
CBHW081210230426
43666CB00015B/2700